ROMANCE DID NOT BEGIN IN ROME

A critique of the Latin origin of Romance languages

Carme Jiménez Huertas

Original title, in Spanish: *No venimos del latín. Edición revisada y ampliada*

© 2016, Carme Jiménez Huertas

Romance Did Not Begin in Rome. A critique of the Latin origin of Romance languages

© 2017, Carme Jiménez Huertas

First Edition, 2013 Editorial Círculo Rojo
Second Edition, 2016 Las Sandalias de Mercurio

Logo design: David Parra
Europe Map by Alexrk2 CC BY-SA 3.0, via Wikimedia Commons
Italy languages Map: SV by Iron_Age_Italy.png: User: Dbachmann derivative work: Ewan ar born (Iron_Age_Italy.png) CC-BY-SA-3.0, via Wikimedia Commons

All rights reserved. No part of this work may be reproduced, stored in a retrieval system, or transmitted in any form or by any means (electronic, mechanical, photocopying, recording or otherwise) without the prior written permission of the copyright owners. Violation of such rights may constitute an offense against intellectual property.

ISBN: 978-1984030214

Printed by CreateSpace

Available from Amazon.com, CreateSpace.com, and other retail outlets

ROMANCE DID NOT BEGIN IN ROME

A critique of the Latin origin of Romance languages

Carme Jiménez Huertas

LAS SANDALIAS DE MERCURIO

ÍNDEX

Foreword by Cristina Brescan VII
Note to the second edition XIII
Acknowledgements XV
Note to the first edition XVII

CHAPTER 1 — 1

1.1 The influence of Latin 1
1.2 Latin - a written language, not a spoken language 2
1.3 What writing did Latin displace? 4
1.4 What language did the Romans speak? 6

CHAPTER 2 — 11

2.1 The sluggishness of linguistic change 11
2.2 The way we think, the way we talk 18

CHAPTER 3 — 21

3.1 The non-existent vulgarization process of Latin 21
3.2 The oldest texts in Romance languages 22
3.3 Similarities between Romance languages 28
3.4 Romans or Romanians? 32
3.5 Features of Latin 38
3.6 From Latin to Vulgar Latin; from proto-Romance to the Romances 40
3.7 Alphabet 44

CHAPTER 4 — 47

4.1 Phonetics 47
4.2 Palatalization 48
4.3 The syllabic structure 50
4.4 The accent 54
4.5 Vocalism 55
4.6 Diphthongs and hiatuses 57
4.7 Consonantism 59

    4.8 Stops (Occlusives) 63

    4.9 Fricatives 64

    4.10 Affricates 66

    4.11 Sonorants 67

    4.12 Consonant groups 68

    4.13 Suppression of sounds 69

    4.14 Addition of sounds 70

CHAPTER 5   73

    5.1 Lexicology 73

    5.2 Etymology 80

    5.3 Toponymy 89

CHAPTER 6   97

    6.1 Morphosyntax 97

    6.2 Morphological generalities in inflected forms 99

    6.3 Nouns 104

    6.4 Adjectives 107

    6.5 Pronouns 107

    6.6 Determiners 111

    6.7 Verbs 115

    6.8 Non-inflected forms: prepositions, adverbs and conjunctions 121

    6.9 Adverbs 122

    6.10 Prepositions 126

    6.11 Conjunctions 128

    6.12 Syntax 133

    6.13 Absence of syntactic function markers (declension) 133

    6.14 Change in the order of sentence constituents 134

    6.15 Interrogative sentences 136

CONCLUSION   139

    Where do Romance languages come from? 139

Foreword

*"First they ignore you,
then they laugh at you,
then they fight you,
then you win."*
Mahatma Gandhi

Dear Readers of the open, wide world,

Do you remember how you felt when you found out you were an adopted child? I assume most of you don't, for a simple reason: you know who your parents are, and that is the truth. Truth be told, I don't remember either – for, in a literal sense, I am not an adopted child. In a literal sense, those of us who have nothing of this kind to remember are lucky.

But, if you are as passionate about history and linguistics as I am, beware: there are experiences out there, symbolic or otherwise, that can leave you just as (if not more) anxious about your identity. Perhaps, even worse, they make you feel unwanted, abandoned, orphaned. And about all this I have a lot to remember.

In 1988, a naïve and enthusiastic student of Romanian at the University of Bucharest was studying for her History of the Romanian Language course. There and then, she had the first opportunity to closely analyze the arguments explaining the birth of Romanian from Latin. Her first suspicions arose when trying to grasp the official historical account of the Romanization process and combine it with the Romanian linguists' general attitude towards the Dacian language. Fair enough, it was expected that one could only develop a rigorous scientific theory if closely guided by available evidence – and there just wasn't enough evidence of the Dacian language, it had not been preserved. In other words, *hardly anything was known* about Dacian, which must have been lost or forgotten. The young student accepted this interpretation at first – until... it got better!

In the Vocabulary of the Romanian language course, only about 150 words were presumed to be of Dacian origin (all in the basic vocabulary, so – not easy to discount). But they were identified as such on the grounds that they could not be classified as being of any other origin. In other words, by elimination. The student found this explanation most unusual, and became curious: what criteria were routinely used to establish the provenance of a word in Romanian? She discovered that, in the vast majority of cases related to the basic vocabulary, if a word was found to exist in other languages, then it was uncritically assumed it must have been borrowed from that language into Romanian. For example, if a Romanian word looked similar to a Latin or Romance word, then it was assumed to have come from Latin (note: not a Romance language, unless it could be specifically identified as a neological borrowing, as was the case for many French words and phrases adopted during the 19th Century, for which documented evidence was available). Where written evidence was not there to assist, the presuppositions used to fill the gaps made very little sense. This was emphatically the case when it came to words of Dacian origin. On the one hand, it was stated that Dacian was unknown. On the other hand, to classify Dacian words through an elimination procedure means to assume that Dacian must have been *completely different* from all the other languages. Surely, one must know a hell of a lot about a language to be able to make such a categorical assumption!

In studying the deep structures of morphology and syntax, the young student found even more evidence converging towards the hypothesis of a Dacian substratum and stratum obliterated by shortcut ascriptions of Latin origins. This student (high school Dux and admitted first in the English-Romanian Philology intake of 1987) went to show her findings and arguments to her Professor of Romanian Grammar. The Professor's reaction was forever imprinted in the student's memory: "Why would I listen to something that goes against everything reputable that has been written on the subject for decades – no, for centuries? How dare you go against what the most reputable researchers of the Romance languages are saying – not only in Romania but also in Italy, Spain and France? Who do you think you are? Why don't you just show some respect for all this arduously acquired scholarship? I urge you: stay away from this false hypothesis if you want to pass the exam."

As she was trying to make a living and find her place in the world, after a battle of conscience the impressionable student took that advice, as follows. First, she graduated (a Dux again) as soon as she could, and resolved there was no place for her to continue studying linguistics in a climate so adverse to intellectual debate, so affected by institutional hierarchy and distance. Then, in 1991, she enrolled in the Bachelor of Arts (Philosophy) degree, the first Program to be cleaned up of old dogmas and become a space for free thinking in post-communist Romania. There she studied logic – initially, just to check that her critique of the Romanization theory had a solid logical foundation. In the process she discovered social, political and moral philosophy – the disciplines she has dedicated her career to ever since. No doubt, her love of philosophy was at first related to its ability to challenge, most profoundly, the dogmatic interpretation her former Professors of

Philology had given to the nature of intellectual inquiry. Supported by a full Australian Government Scholarship, she completed a PhD in Philosophy at the University of Melbourne in 2005. She is now co-Leader of a Sustainability Research Group and Senior Lecturer in Philosophy and Ethics (Management and Organization) at the ARWU[1]-ranked Swinburne University in Melbourne, guiding MBA students (society's leaders of today and tomorrow) on how to think. She is also trying to give her students as many opportunities for reasonable, open, fair and equal intellectual debate as possible.

In 2016, alerted by colleagues from Romania, the former young student discovered the arguments put forward by Carme Jimenez Huertas in *No venimos del latin*; read (breathlessly) everything she could find online about this work; and wrote to Ms Huertas to express her gratitude. A rich intellectual dialogue ensued, and she is now writing this **Foreword**.

So let me explain, in a less personal way, why the hypotheses documented by Ms Huertas in this book are ground-breaking.

First, they urge us to significantly modify our time horizon, our understanding of chronologies and timespans, when it comes to language development at community level. I dare say, this is on a par with shifting the estimation of geological eras (the formation of the earth) from cca 75,000 years (Buffon, 18th Century) to the order of billions (20th Century). In this respect, historical linguistics has a lot of catching up to do, philosophically and methodologically.

Secondly, it places not only Catalan (or Romanian) but all Romance languages in a more plausible and natural relationship with their ancestry, with Latin, and with each other.

Thirdly, it confers the domination of the Roman Empire a more plausible role, at least from a linguistic perspective. In the case of Dacia, the Roman Conquest may have (at most) led to influences similar to that of French over Romanian in the 19th Century but not to overhauls or complete replacements. Especially in the Western Romance space, it is more natural to assume that Latin may have exercised more influence when dead rather than alive, due to the universalizing religious, political and cultural function it was conferred in medieval Europe, as well as to later metamorphoses.

Fourthly, here is a starting point to formulate a clear sense in which Romanians and the Romanian language are not alone, not an odd and idiosyncratic

---

[1] Every year, the Academic Ranking of World Universities (ARWU), the world's leading university ranking system, based at the Shanghai Jiao-Tong University (China), assesses and ranks the top 500 universities globally.

phenomenon, not an accident of history, not an enigma and not a miracle (if allowed to continue his work, the unfortunate Gh. I. Brătianu[2] may have reached the same conclusion). Romance peoples are sharing an important quest for their linguistic origins.

And now I come to the fifth point I have to make – I believe, the most important of all: the work in this book does more than bring to us, for analysis, a body of evidence in support of an unsettling hypothesis. It questions some of the most fundamental premises in mainstream linguistic methodology, and in historical linguistics in particular. In doing so, it encourages (explicitly or implicitly) a different understanding and practice of linguistics. Here is a brief outline of this different set of principles:

1. The deep structure[3] of a language is in a mutual relationship of reflection, support and influence with the structure of thought. This suggests that assumptions about the evolution of languages should be enriched by findings from (for example) neurolinguistics and cognitive science;

2. The deep structure of a language is stable, continuing, conservative and non-hybrid, hence evolution and innovation at this level are much slower than in the surface structure;

3. Where evidence is open to interpretation (which, as a genuine linguist knows, happens most of the time), the principles of *plausibility* and *simplicity* should prevail. Both principles, highly regarded within the scientific method of the natural sciences, converge towards the same lesson: among multiple mutually exclusive explanations, the one that provides the most natural interpretation for most data, without the need for additional (convoluted or disruptive) explanations, should be favoured;

---

2 Gh. I. Brătianu (1898-1953) was a Romanian historian, Professor at the 'Alexandru Ioan Cuza' University of Iaşi, one of the last politically active members of the Brătianu family, whose contribution to the national-liberal politics of modern Romania is of exceptional significance. He authored *O enigmă şi un miracol istoric: poporul român* (Engl. *An Enigma and a Historical Miracle: The Romanian People*), published by King Carol II Foundation for Literature and Art in 1940. Arrested by the Communists in 1947 and incarcerated without trial in 1950, he died in the horrific Sighet Prison in 1953.

3 Originally defined by Noam Chomsky (see *Syntactic Structures*, 1957), the concepts of deep and surface structure are fundamental to understanding the generative and transformational features of a language and its grammatical system. The concept of deep structure, in particular, makes an important connection between linguistic and logical structures – although it now requires a lot more refinement, in light of recent discoveries in neurolinguistics.

4. Where there is no evidence (archaeological or otherwise) of traumatic disruption in culture, the principle of *linguistic continuity* should prevail; and

5. Relying on closed systems (such as highly institutionalized written languages) to explain the historical evolution of open systems (such as natural living languages) is unlikely to increase explanatory power – so the bases for analysis and evolutionary explanation should be sought elsewhere (for example, in the spoken idioms of surviving traditionalist communities).

Ms Huertas' study is therefore not only a book of achievements but also one of openings. For even if it turns out that some of the examples given here may end up receiving other explanations later on, the underlying gain (the revolutionary perspective it proposes) remains.

On this note, let me make two addresses – to the linguists of today, and to those to be.

Dear Professors of the official Chairs of Historical Romance Linguistics, the 'ignore' and 'laugh at' phases have passed. Those who challenge the mainstream wisdom are not after your Chairs: they only claim an open, public level of intellectual debate, under whose reasonable principles we are all equal. This is the new space where the real game is played. If you wish to support Romanization theory, then the burden of proof is on you to evidence and argue its plausibility.

Dear students of Historical Romance Linguistics, try to forget what you have been told in a 19th Century-looking 21st Century classroom about what and how to reflect on languages of the past. As difficult as it may seem, try to 'experience' the old languages and cultures you are studying, by activating your most intimate linguistic sensibilities and intuitions, by contemplating the most original evidence – and, from that standpoint, try to develop a sense of direction about what *you think* this evidence is telling you. Write your hypotheses down quickly, then take a break and have a good rest. When you return to your notes, put your analytical philosopher's hat on, check the strength of your concepts and principles, and prepare the best argument possible, based on what you have. Then be ready to interact with proponents of alternative interpretations. Do not accept any alternative premises without reasonable justification (appeals to authority would not do). Verify that the explanations you do receive are indeed better than yours, based on sound methodological criteria, as well as on criteria of reasonable, open, fair and equal intellectual debate. If they are better, carefully adjust your beliefs to give them justice. If they are not, have the courage to request more rigour from your interlocutors, making your criteria and expectations explicit. Whatever path you choose, be assertive. Do not behave like the 19-year old Romanian student who did not know how to stand her ground when it mattered most.

And now let me close with a brief note on how the English title of Ms Huertas' book came about. During one of our conversations, she expressed concern that the literal English translation (*We do not come from Latin*) would be problematic because the audience, and therefore the referent of 'we', had changed. As I was following her line of thought, I realized it was time for a different referent in terms of imagery as well. Back to the drawing board – what was the single most important message this book was set to convey to the new, especially non-Romance, public? That Romance languages do not come from Latin. 'But why are they called Romance then?', I could easily imagine a schoolchild asking. So the coin dropped: the identity issue must be exposed from the very start, from the title itself – questioning the very name of 'Romance'. This English solution is also attractive because, if only for a fleeting moment, it holds the scent of a Romantic novel – another mislabelled identity in need of redress. Both hints converge towards the same suggestion: all is not what it seems. Dear reader, lift that veil from your eyes! Which veil? The one you did not realize was there, the veil of your most stable belief. Like in a Confucian ritual, it is first necessary to rectify names.

It has been a delight and a privilege for me to read Carme Huertas' work, speak with her, and offer suggestions for minor improvements of the English version. I hope you will enjoy the intellectual and emotional experience of reading this book at least as much as I have.

Cristina Brescan
Melbourne, Australia
3 December 2017

Note to the second edition

This book is the second edition of the original work I presented in *No venimos del latin* (literally translated as *We do not come from Latin*). It is not a reprint but an enlargement. Unlike the first edition, where more questions than answers were left in the air, this new work presents my research hypotheses.

After the first edition *tin* and my interview with the journalist Alish, published on YouTube, I received many emails. Some were very critical. However, an increasing number of people were contacting me not only with messages of support but also to provide extra information relevant to my research. In their emails, they provided information that I did not know about, specified or added information, forwarded references and links to videos, photographs, and so on.

The names of some of these contributors are in the body of the text or in the footnotes. However, it is impossible for me to mention them all, so I want to take this opportunity to express my appreciation for each and every one of these small contributions that have encouraged me to print a new edition including some of these comments.

Another important development in this edition is the incorporation of the Romanian language. The hypothesis of a parent tongue prior to the so-called Romanization thus acquires much more strength and consistency. The Romans only occupied Dacia for 165 years and during this period they conquered less than a quarter of the territories lying north of Danube where the Romanian language has been spoken. The other Romanization agents found in the rest of the countries where Romance languages were spoken did not occur in Romania[1]. So how can it be that the Romanian language occupies a much larger territory and has survived so many tough, non-Romance subsequent invasions? The structural, lexical, phonetic and conceptual similarities between Romanian and the rest of Romance languages —distant languages whose peoples have not been in contact for the last two thousand years— point to a common ancestor, an agglutinative and compositional language from which the so-called Romance languages would stem. The evidence is increasingly conclusive: this process does not originate in Latin.

---

[1] In the case of Romanian, Latin was not a scholarly language. We will expand on this topic when we discuss the Romanization agents.

Acknowledgements

I wish to express my deepest gratitude and friendship to Alícia Ninou, an independent journalist, for her faith in my research and for encouraging me to have it published without fearing the reaction. Her journalistic work is a beacon of reference.

In a very special way, I wish to thank philologist Núria Garcia Quera, my research colleague, for her friendship. For many years we have had lengthy conversations on linguistics that materialized into projects, giving shape to suggestive new hypotheses.

Deep gratitude also goes to Mihaela Alda, for her professionalism, and for enabling me to discover the Romanian language and culture. She provided me with 'the missing link'.

I do greatly appreciate the support and presence of all the members of the group *Amics dels Ibers*, in Terrassa, and the group *Euskararen Jatorria*, for sharing their passion for the language and culture of our ancestors.

I would also like to express my sincere gratitude to all Romanians who have contacted me providing information and references. Among the many, I would like to mention the anonymous *East Man* who translated into Romanian the subtitles of the interview posted on YouTube, and Dumitru Sonea, who edited and improved them, synchronizing them with the voice; Laur Ionescu, Alex S.H. Abaci and Marian Voicu, who shed light on the history of Dacia; to Ovidiu Someșan, for his revision of the Romanian version of the text and to Daniel Roxin, promoter of the translation and publication of this material in Romanian, without whose collaboration and encouragement the Romanian edition would not have been possible.

Last but not least, I am very grateful to Cristina Brescan. When I was pushed through the storm by the hardest attacks of criticism and academic opposition, feeling like a castaway on a lost island, a bottle with a message of hope appeared on the sand beach. I received an email that came from the other end of the world. Literally, Australia is at the antipodes of Spain. I had never imagined that help would come from so far.

In her letter, Cristina Brescan told me she had studied linguistics at the University of Bucharest. Having researched the premises of the Romanization theory, she began to question the logic of some of the arguments taught. As soon as she suggested a possible inaccuracy of some topics to her professor, she was stopped by the rigidity of a system that does not admit dissent. She understood that «the mainstream mentality could not produce significant change in knowledge, simply because no significant change can result from being conventional. The price paid in academic freedom is increasingly high». Cristina Brescan is currently teaching Philosophy of Research (to PhD students), Ethics, and Strategy (to MBA students). She has dedicated almost thirty years to helping students use criteria beyond what mainstream mentality defends. She has become a great advocate of critical thinking, so it is an honor for me that she has agreed to write the prologue for this book.

Cristina is the professor that every good student would need to find.

She was the one who encouraged me to translate this book into English. She has read and reviewed the text, and has raised points to be deepened with new research. Her help is invaluable. I am very grateful for her time, knowledge and friendship – and also because she helped me understand how the logic of truth can be so strong that it goes around the world.

Note to the first edition

> *Odi et amo. Quare id faciam? fortasse requiris. /*
> *Nescio, sed fieri sentio et excrucior.*
> «I hate and I love. Why do I do this, perhaps you ask. /
> I do not know, but I feel it happening and I am tortured ».
>
> Gayus Valerius Catullus (87 - 57 BC)

For many years, in schools and universities, we have been taught that Romance languages come from Latin. Following the axiom or unquestioned principle that Latin was the parent tongue, solutions to explain linguistic changes were sought using Latin as a starting point. Historical grammar has described this process on the basis of successive changes that would have caused a deep transformation of the parent tongue, which degenerated into the so-called Vulgar Latin, and which in turn, through new and sometimes complicated changes, formed the Romance languages. These are, in alphabetical order: Catalan, French, Galician, Italian, Occitan, Romanian, Romansh, Sardinian, and Spanish.

As Romance languages would be the result of a degeneration of Latin, they have been studied as members of the same family, whose parent tongue was Latin. Hence, it is expected that they should resemble Latin as much as they do their sister tongues, since they all would have departed, following different paths, from the centre of the original Latin grammar. And yet, that is not what we find. In fact, the opposite is true: Romance languages are too much like each other. Even those that seem to be far removed, such as Galician and Romanian, through this supposed degeneration have come to identical solutions. This is when we begin to ask ourselves whether traditional teachings provide an adequate explanation of the relationship between Romance languages, and whether this relationship is really established by original reference to Latin.

Once this fundamental assumption is challenged, many others questions inevitably arise.

For although it is true that many words from Romance languages exist in Latin, often these words are also found, and with few differences, in English and German. It even happens that we find the same word in all Romance languages except in Latin, from which it is supposed to have stemmed. And after a more thorough analysis, if we look at the morphology and syntax, the differences from the so-called parent tongue are even more evident, with the added paradox that the different Romance languages coincide again in the solutions adopted. They diverge from Latin and converge with each other, i.e. they move away from the so-called parent tongue and are united together, defending a new hypothesis of a common origin that does not necessarily go through Latin.

It is inevitable to ask ourselves how it is possible that until now it has not been questioned that Latin was the parent tongue of Romance languages.[1]

In this brief study, I will contribute arguments based on linguistic evidence in order to open a debate on the origin, evolution and degree of kinship of Romance languages and Latin.

---

1 During the Renaissance, there was a theory in France that argued a Greek origin of French: TRIPPAULT, LÉON. *Celt'-hellenisme ou, Etymologic des mots françois tirez du grœc. Plus. Preuves en general de la descente de nostre langue. Par Leon Trippault, sieur de Bardis.* Orleans (1581). Text available at the Lyon Library, at:

http://catalogue.bm-lyon.fr/?fn=Search&q=%20(%20au%3Dtrippault+leon%20)%20

CHAPTER 1

1.1 The influence of Latin

My initial reflection in this chapter defends the importance of Latin. Its widespread influence cannot be disregarded.

For many centuries Latin has been a (if not 'the') scholarly language in half of Europe. What is the meaning of a scholarly language? It is a language used in the Humanities, for the study of linguistics, law, history, religion and literature. Latin and Greek were very important in the formation of neologisms and learned terms, as well as in the word composition and derivation processes. Both languages helped to create many new words and precise terminology to define the new concepts that came with social and cultural changes as well as new knowledge. For example, Latin is still the language used for designating biological categories in the International Code of Botanical Nomenclature.

Throughout the Middle Ages, Latin's importance was paramount because it functioned as the only written language. Its study gained new strength during the Renaissance and modernity. For example, it was still used by scientists such as Nicholas Copernicus and Isaac Newton. The very definition of Classical Latin as a scholarly language implies a contrast with Vulgar Latin: while the former was a language of erudition, to which common people had no access, the latter was the language of the masses (vulgus) or the uneducated. Plebeians –the people, or third state, i.e. those who were not part of the 'gens' or privileged classes of the nobility and clergy– had no access to culture and did not understand Latin.

And how did a dead language become a scholarly language? This is a good question; no sooner have we asked it than the answer arises almost automatically. There was an intention in adopting Latin as a written language when there were no longer any native speakers. Latin was neither spoken nor understood, unless it was studied. The answer to this question is that Latin was the language of power. It was the language used in the liturgy of the Catholic Church and in the royal chancelleries.[1]

---

1 In this case, the exception was Romania. Most Romanians have always belonged to the Orthodox Church and, according to Laur Ionescu and other comments received, the language of the Church had more influences from Greek and Slavonic than from Latin.

The use of Latin as a scholarly language was very scarce. At the end of the 18th Century, the Transylvanian School led a latinizing cultural movement that had a great influence on the later evolution of Romanian (Mihaela Alda).

Latin was chosen to apply a three-strata social structure that divided society into classes based upon economic criteria:

- Priests and Nobility
- Knights
- Peasants and Traders

Based upon the religious ideology of the Catholic Church, social stratification was applied according to the criteria of feudalism and its ruling class. This choice was no accident and its success has been maintained to this day.

Hence, this situation was not the result of a degeneration of the Latin language into a vulgar language, a clearly derogatory term. There is too much evidence indicating that Vulgar Latin did not exist. Had it existed, we should find many more 'intermediate links' written in this 'degenerated' Latin rather than in the Romance languages, and yet this is not so. Written Latin is always Classical Latin: it does not evolve beyond the personal expertise of the person who uses a dead language. However, Romance languages appear to be quite well defined from the very first texts.

This should make us think.

Perhaps it is time we got rid of imposed assumptions that cannot be explained on purely linguistic grounds, thus being detrimental to our fundamental understanding of the natural evolution of languages.

1.2 Latin - a written language, not a spoken language

Let us reflect for a moment on an important point: Latin was a written language, not a spoken one.

Speaking in one language and writing in another is very frequent. This situation is much more common than it may seem. It happened for example with Hieratic, Demotic and Coptic Egyptian language. In ancient Egypt, three types of script were developed: the oldest form was the hieroglyphic script or sacred characters from 3200 BC, reserved for use and understanding by the higher castes, for rituals with religious purposes. Hieroglyphs were carved on tablets, temple walls, papyrus, and ostraca or stone flakes. Over time, there emerged a hieratic script, a stylized form of hieroglyphic writing. Later, a demotic script was invented as a stylized form of the hieratic script and was used on stone or wood for commercial contracts and literary writings. Between 650 and 400 BC it was used in administrative, legal and commercial texts, while hieroglyphic and hieratic writing continued to be used solely for ceremonial texts.

> **Latin as the key to understanding a world foregone, not to be spoken**
>
> "Here is where the big difference between teaching classical languages and living languages originates. The former are taught in faculties and colleges where great importance is given to philology; if their study is reinforced by the knowledge of the history and literature of ancient peoples, then it will acquire a philosophical character that can only be appreciated by young people whose intelligence has been prepared for high ideas. On the contrary, living languages are almost always studied by younger learners; they are part of the elementary education considered either as a fundament for further knowledge, or as a study of useful and immediate application.
>
> For this reason, and because the teaching of the languages has a certain distinctiveness which cannot be overlooked, in those countries where it is carried out in official institutions, they always try to submit it to prescriptions favouring exclusively practical systems and methods."
> (Anonymous, *Legislative collection of elementary education*, Alicante, Cervantes Virtual Library-University of Alicante, 2003).

In later stages, in the Ptolemaic era, the increased use of Demotic script became the official script, with the paradox that the writing represented the Demotic language, a variety of the Egyptian language that was no longer spoken because the language had been diverging, being progressively replaced by the Greek language and Coptic writing. And yet the Demotic writing continued to be in use until the year 450 AD (temple of Isis in Philae). The simultaneous use of the three scripts (Hieroglyphic, Demotic, and ancient Greek) in the trilingual text of the Rosetta Stone was precisely what enabled us to decipher the hitherto unintelligible Egyptian hieroglyphic script. The texts written in Late Demotic script have an artificial or even contrived character, with a clear parallel in the case at hand: Classical Latin written when the Latin language was already a dead language.

The Egyptian example is not singular. A similar case occurred between Hebrew and Aramaic. And previously, with Akkadian and cuneiform script derived from Sumerian: the former being a Semitic language spoken by Assyrians and Babylonians and even used in writings between Egyptian pharaohs and Hittite kings.

The division between spoken and written languages did not only occur in remote times. It can be said that this situation continues to occur now in many parts of the world. Such is the case, for example, with Arabic and Mandarin Chinese.

Have you noticed how in Chinese markets people often use a slate for negotiations before closing a deal? They are writing the characters in Mandarin Chinese. They share a common writing although they do not understand each other when they speak (there are more than a hundred different languages spoken in China!).

Also, many of the indigenous languages in Africa and America have no writing. Their culture has been orally transmitted and no written records have been left. Colonialism contributed to this in the schools created by the colonizers. These schools taught all children to write in Spanish, English and French, disregarding the local languages of the inhabitants. When the colonies regained their independence, vernacular languages were recovered, but in most cases they did not develop their own writing and started using the alphabets of colonizers for writing, in particular the Latin alphabet. Islamic countries chose to use Arabic script or its Urdu adaptation, and in Hindu countries the Devanagari alphabet was chosen. However, the influence of the imperialist languages has been so great that they are not only still the first or second language, but in many cases continue to be the only written language.

All this helps us to understand that speaking in one language and writing in another has been, and still is, quite common.

1.3 What writing did Latin displace?

In the Iberian Peninsula, Latin displaced Iberian as a written language.

However, it is important to explain that this was not achieved by the Ancient Romans but by the Church later on. Latin became the written language of the Western Catholic Church, while the Eastern Orthodox Church maintained the use of Greek.

Why do we say that Latin was not implemented by the Romans? Because, under full Roman rule, not only did Iberian script not disappear but it actually spread, expanding its area of influence. Why? We should ask ourselves this question!

Imagine the situation for a moment. On the Iberian Peninsula, several scripts were used. We will focus on the Northeastern Iberian script (hereafter called Iberian). Iberian writing is found on all kinds of supports and contexts, from pottery and household utensils to lead plaques, transport amphoras, loom weights, cultic containers found in funerary contexts, rock inscriptions, coins, mosaics, bronze plaques with public announcements, prayers and invocations to protective deities, and many more. Therefore, it was not a skill restricted to an elite but a knowledge with a broad social distribution. Archaeological findings with scripture are diverse and plentiful, exceeding four thousand units and therefore this is one of the few scripts with such a wide and extensive inventory which has so far resisted decipherment.

The Iberian script had been consolidated since the 7th Century BC. Its writing was probably prior to this, as such a complex system does not just appear out of the blue. However, when the writing recipients were labile, such as leather or parchment, they were not preserved; only non-perishable recipients such as stones, ceramic or lead survived. Therefore, we will start with the chronology provided and determined by the archaeological context in which the texts were discovered, with the lead plaques of Ullastret being among the oldest.

The Iberian script is semi-syllabic, mixing characters with alphabetical value (sonant vowels and consonants) and others with syllabic value (occlusive consonants). According to Gómez Moreno[2], Iberian writing has a distinctly archaic character. Due to its structure, the basic signary contains around 30 characters (15 alphabetic signs and 15 syllabic signs), it is halfway between syllabaries and alphabets, because when a script evolves, technically it tends to reduce the total number of characters necessary for the written representation of a language.

This writing is around three hundred years older than the arrival of the Romans. Before the Romans, the Greeks and Phoenicians also used their own scripts. Thus we have that Phoenicians, Greeks and Romans used alphabetic writings and yet never managed to displace the use of the Iberian syllabic writing, which spread to other geographic areas and, against all odds, remained alive until the 1st or 2nd century AD.

The Iberian script was adopted by Celtic and Celtiberian peoples under Roman rule. Why? It is a good question. If there is a simplified alphabetical system, why use a more complex syllabic system that makes it difficult to transcribe consonant groups? The premises used in the mainstream interpretations of these phenomena have to be re-thought and revised!

If the bronze plaques from Botorrita dating to the 1st Century BC (found at the site of Contrebia Belaisca, Botorrita, Zaragoza) and the bronze from Luzaga (Guadalajara) among others are written in Iberian script, this means that:

---

[2] Manuel Gómez-Moreno Martínez (1870-1970), a Spanish archaeologist and historian, a member of the Spanish Royal Academy (RAE), one of the pioneers in the study of Iberian writing.

- It was a script that Celtiberians understood and therefore could read. It was known to them, because it was already established and used by their Iberian neighbours.
- Someone was 'still' speaking this language, otherwise they would not voluntarily have used the signary of a dead or unknown language (especially that of the Romans, who were the invaders).
- Faced with the dilemma of writing in Latin or in Iberian, if it so happened that there was such a choice, the latter was chosen and, more importantly, the Romans accepted this naturally, the same as they had accepted that the Greeks and Phoenicians, albeit under Roman rule, would use their own scripts.

The Iberian script was used until the time of Augustus, in the 1st Century AD. After that, the Iberian language ceased to be written but did not cease to be spoken.

Sometimes we do not take into account that the Romans were conquerors who applied imperialistic policies and that, having gained supremacy on the Iberian Peninsula, were the ones writing the history. We will cite a few words from the Greek historian Polybius (200-120 BC), a specialist in military strategy and technique, who accompanied Scipio on one of his expeditions to Spain: "This is Rome's policy: it acts with such agility that it would appear to be the benefactor of the peoples it submits."[3]

1.4 What language did the Romans speak?

The soldiers of the Roman legions of Hispania did not speak Latin.

We should not find this surprising: I will explain why. First, the Italian peninsula was inhabited by different peoples, divided into three major linguistic groups:

- The Latino-Faliscan languages: Faliscan was spoken north of the city of Rome, while Latin was spoken in the Lazio region, in the centre of Italy.
- The Osco-Umbrian or Sabellian languages: Oscan was spoken in central and southern Italy. Due to their proximity, Marrucinian, Paelignian and Vestinian are considered its dialects. Umbrian was spoken in the central-northern region and included the following dialects: Marsian, Sabine, Aequian, Volscian and Ernician. South Picene was spoken in the central Adriatic region and is characterized by its inventory of seven

---

3 Quoted from MARTÍ I CASTELL, JOAN, *Gramàtica històrica catalana I. Els orígens de la llengua*. UOC (1999) p. 13

vowels. A variant called North Picene does not appear to be an Indo-European language and is linked to Etruscan.

- Tyrrhenian languages: Etruscan, spoken in Tuscany. It is thought to have disappeared due to the decline of the Etruscan civilization in 200 BC. It was absorbed by Latin, which maintained only a dozen of its words. Rhaetian and Lemnian also belong to the same Tyrrhenian family of languages.

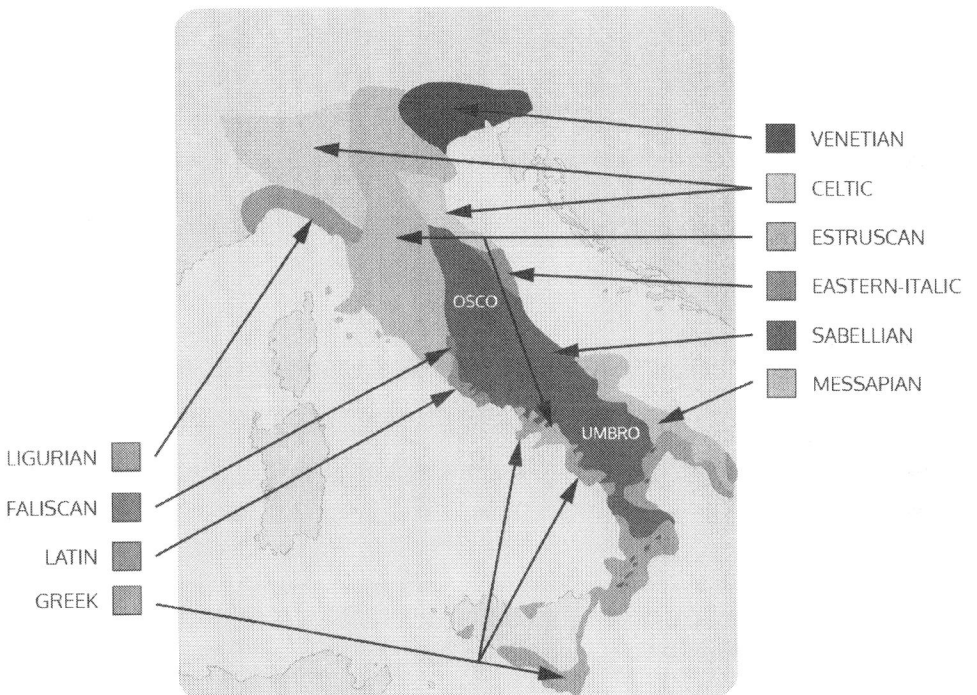

Source: http://www.unizar.es/hant/Roma/italialenguas.html

When, in the course of the 7th Century BC, Rome's influence extended beyond the region of Lazio, it found two major flourishing cultures: Etruscan in the north, and Greek in the south. Both had a huge impact on Roman culture and both were using their own writing, different from the Latin one - as we shall see when we speak about the Latin alphabet (Chapter 3.7).

Many authors question the existence of a common Italic. Although different languages share grammatical or phonetic similarities, these could be caused by their geographical proximity or by a convergent development of languages belonging to different families. Looking at the map, one can appreciate the insignificant extension of the Latin-Phaliscan languages compared to the non-Indo-European languages: Etruscan on the one hand, and Sabellian languages on the other. Even Greek seems to have more presence in the Italic peninsula than Latin.

Rome had subdued all the populations and used auxiliary Italic troops in its campaigns of conquest, consisting of soldiers from all regions of the empire. This explains why there were so many different languages in the Roman legionary. Therefore, the idea of an educated army speaking only Latin does not conform to reality.

Another issue to consider is that some sources indicate that Latin was a dead language in the 3rd century BC. There is the following epitaph on the gravestone of poet Gneaeus Naevius, who died in 201 BC:

> *Immortales mortales si foret fas flere,*
> *flerent diuae Camenae Naeuium poetam,*
> *itaque, postquam est Orchi traditus thesauro,*
> *obliti sunt Romani loquier lingua Latina.*[4]

Naevius's epic, the *Bellum Poenicum* (Punic War), written in Saturnian metre and evoking for the first time the legends of the founding of Rome, was the first manifestation of Latin epic poetry. His style was considered archaic, vulgar and not very elegant, a curious detail because, although the authors of the next generations mentioned and praised the poem, it was not for its poetic value, but because it celebrated the national glories.

Virgil, Ovid, Cicero, and even Horace, who was the son of a freed slave, received a first class education. Much has been debated about whether the refined style of Cicero's was the same language as that spoken by the Romans. It is said that, as a writer, he gave Latin an abstract lexicon which it lacked; and he transferred and translated many terms from Greek, thus transforming Latin into a scholarly language, suitable for expressing deeper thought. Cicero's prose was then the model that established as Classical Latin. Was this scholarly Latin the same language as the one in which Naevius wrote – that is, a language described as archaic and vulgar?

---

4 If immortals were allowed to weep for mortals, the divine Muses would weep for the poet Naevius. And so after he was delivered to the strongbox of Orchus, Romans forgot how to speak the Latin language.

Lastly, another question arises. How is it possible that during the classical period it was necessary to study Latin grammar and Latin rhetoric in the same way as Greek was studied? Why the obsession with copying Greek lyrics, themes and metrics? Why the persistent contrast between the written word (considered to have prestige) and the oral discourse (considered prosaic eloquence)? Why was the latter deemed less versatile, while the former always required taking lessons to master it?

Time and again it has been shown that, except for the patricians, the Romans had to study to speak Latin correctly. The reason can be found in the fact that, given the mixture of Italic languages spoken, some unification and standardization were necessary, as with the dialectal variables of some modern languages. Classical Latin would be the written language resulting from this homogenization. However, for speaking, everyone would use their own mother tongue, a language they themselves referred to as *romana lingua*.

It seems increasingly evident that Latin was nobody's native language but rather a language in which they could all understand each other. In a first stage it was a planned and imposed language, enabling military leaders to address the troops and promote unity among armies of different origins, legislators and scholars to draft legal, historical and literary documents, to validate political agreements and commercial contracts in an intelligible way for all, and to spread knowledge. Later, this imposition continued with the resurgence of Latin culture and arts directed by the Catholic Church, establishing a common identity under the Holy Roman Empire of Germany...[5]

Returning to the Iberian Peninsula, the contingent of colonizers came from the central and southern regions of the Italian peninsula and spoke Sabellian languages from the Osco-Umbrian family. Furthermore, it should be noted that, since the Punic Wars, the Roman armies located in Hispania employed

---

5 I would like to include in this new edition the commentary of reader Guillem Nicolàs i Larruy, a speaker of Esperanto, a language constructed by the Polish ophthalmologist L.L. Zamenhof. Esperanto is a language with 80-90% of Greco-Roman roots created with the purpose of acting as a bridge between cultures and speakers of different languages. Zamenhof spoke Greek, Latin, French, German, Polish, Russian and Yiddish. It is for this reason that Esperanto is based on words common to most of these languages. The interesting thing about this reasoning is the possible parallelism between Cicero's Latin and Zamenhof's Esperanto. If that were true, Latin would not be the parent tongue of Romance languages, but the opposite: Romance languages would be the parent languages of Latin in the same way as Greek, Latin, French, German, Polish, Russian, and Yiddish are the parents of Esperanto. This would explain the imposition of a language with little phonetic richness and a simplified alphabet, which cannot reliably represent any of the living languages it stems from but which is useful for shared communications precisely because it is based upon elements common to all these living languages.

citizens from inland villages of the Peninsula as auxiliaries to the Roman legions, against both the Carthaginians and other peoples on the Peninsula. Only the senior officers learned Latin, Greek or Phoenician, which is why they cannot be considered as active agents of Romanization.

Therefore, if the soldiers of the Roman armies of Hispania, a mixed group of Italics and Hispanics, cannot be considered active agents of Romanization, where are the thousands of people who disseminated their language, devastating all languages from the big cities to the most remote mountain valleys? At that time, there was certainly no public or compulsory education, TV policies or language immersion. How did the Roman legions manage to get illiterate peasants, fishermen, miners, artisans or shepherds to cease speaking their mother tongues in favour of Cicero's Latin, a language Romans themselves needed years to master?

Things may not have happened as we were led to believe!

CHAPTER 2

2.1 The sluggishness of linguistic change

If the Romans did not speak Latin, how is it possible to assert that the inhabitants of our lands replaced their mother tongue with a language they did not understand; or, worse, that they began to speak it so badly that they lost their grammatical cases and genders along the way? How could this new language have been so different from Latin that it would not be understood? And for all these changes to occur in four hundred years only? There are too many unanswered questions: this is because the explanations given to justify the linguistic changes from Latin are not satisfactory. In fact, they *do not* answer the questions raised here.

Could there be another explanation?

Let us first look at what has happened with other Mediterranean languages. For instance, if we compare Ancient and Modern Greek (or Old and Modern Turkish, or Old and Modern Arabic), there is not as much distance as between Latin and the so-called Romance languages.

If the distance between modern and ancient languages is so small, it means that the processes linguistic transformations, within the same language, do not occur from one generation to the next by 'spontaneous mutation'. We are referring specifically to internal changes (i.e. to the evolution of a language from within, using internal resources) rather than external changes (i.e. based on influences from outside) – and this aspect is essential. Languages evolve internally at a slow or very slow pace, as we shall see immediately below. Only abrupt external changes justify a rapid change, such as a contact that compels two different cultures to communicate, i.e. due to conquest or trade. As a result of the sum of two very distant languages, a new language can emerge that blends elements from both languages, as happened with Creole. But even in such exceptional situations, we must specify what part of each language is present in the new language and how the transmission occurs between generations. Linguists do not agree on this point: although in Creole there may be an important lexicon transfer, the syntax must clearly belong to one of the two languages. A pidgin, as these lingua franca codes are often called, stems from the need for speakers of two different languages to communicate. When due to grammatical distance, the two different populations cannot find a generalized and accessible interlanguage, pidgin provides a basic and simple means in communication but in no case does it become the mother tongue of a community. Typically, language transmission occurs from mother to child in fully developed form. This was checked in the case of bilingual families: both languages are incorporated naturally without tending to create hybrids. Languages do not lose their form or become de-structured syntactically; they maintain their rules and nobody stops conjugating verbs. In situations of extreme diglossia, especially in adulthood, a speaker can transfer elements from the dominant language, and even change one mother tongue for another, due to the need to communicate with speakers of other languages. These changes usually occur externally, by imposition of a dominant language, and require support from a rapid process, to be able to compete with mothers passing on language to their children, whatever it may be, in a perfectly structured way. All this confirms the views of Jesús Tusón[6], who states that a language only disappears when its speakers stop using it and replace it with that of the ruling class. There are no linguistic reasons for this – but only political, social or cultural reasons.

Contrary to external change, internal change is slow or very slow. Mark Pagel[7], a professor of evolutionary biology, and his colleagues at the University of Reading in Britain have built a statistical model to show that some words from European languages have remained in use for more than 15,000 years. They are called 'protowords' and are quite often the most common words: they have been transmitted with such fidelity that we can recognize them. This allows researchers to work on a hypothetical reconstruction of this alleged 'super language family' that would be the common ancestor of seven language families and some 700 modern languages, equivalent to 10% of the languages spoken in the world. This new statistical model is really fascinating, for although we are aware that we cannot just rely on figures when investigating linguistic change, it does provide a map of what might have happened. For example, it allows us to determine that only 50% of words change or are replaced in a period ranging from 2000 to 4000 years, while others withstand change for 15,000 years or more. Which words are most commonly maintained? Words used in everyday speech with a frequency of more than once per thousand words. And which are they? Numbers, pronouns and adverbs, but also very commonly used words like *man*, *fire* and *mother*. Researchers even show complete sentences that we can still understand today.

---

6   Jesús Tusón Valls was a professor at the University of Barcelona Faculty of Philology and founder of the first Linguistics Department in Spain.

7   Link to the publication: http://www.pnas.org/content/early/2013/05/01/1218726110

The following table shows 23 words that have a common ancestor in seven Eurasian language families:

Meaning	Cognate class size *	Frequency of use #	Part of speech
Thou	7	2,524	Pronoun
I	6	4,332	Pronoun
Not	5	7,602	Adverb
That	5	5,846	Adjective
We	5	2,956	Pronoun
To give	5	1,606	Verb
Who	5	1,172	Pronoun
This	4	11,185	Adjective
What	4	2,058	Adverb
Man/Male	4	2,800	Noun
Ye	4	1,459	Pronoun
Old	4	746	Adjective
Mother	4	717	Noun
To hear	4	680	Verb
Hand	4	658	Noun
Fire	4	398	Noun
To pull	4	279	Verb
Black	4	135	Adjective
To flow	4	91	Verb
Bark	4	49	Noun
Ashes	4	23	Noun
To spit	4	23	Verb
Worm	4	21	Noun

* Defined as the number (out of seven) Eurasiatic language families that are reconstructed as cognate for the word used to convey the meaning shown

\# The frequency of use per million based on mean of 17 languages from six language families and two isolates (16)

Source: http://terraeantiqvae.com

In the previous table, we can see that the most frequently used word is *this* (11,185), followed by *not* (7,602) and *that* (5,846). Included in the grammatical category of 'adjectives' are the determiners, which in Spanish are grouped in an independent category as they can be used as adjectives or pronouns. It is important to point out that the words most resistant to change are precisely two closed categories: pronouns and adverbs[8]. We should remember this as we will come back to it later.

Although it may seem that we have moved away from the subject, it is not so. We were trying to demonstrate that internal linguistic changes take not centuries but millennia to occur. It is clear that words evolve, as we can see from the Latin *pater* and the English *father*, establishing a regular transformation from / P / to / F / between these two languages.

An interesting example of the slowness of linguistic change is the fact that the English, Portuguese and Spanish spoken by the Europeans travelling to the Americas in the 15th Century are not so far removed today from the languages of the old continent. In fact, Americans speak English, Brazilians speak Portuguese and Latin Americans speak Spanish: in five hundred years there has been very little evolution in these languages, and speakers on both sides of the Atlantic can easily communicate.

All the present forms of Spanish stem from the early modern or classical Spanish.[9] The changes from classical to modern Spanish are in the prosody (accent, intonation and loss of voiced sibilants), in the fixation of clitic pronouns, and in the equalization of composite forms of unergative and unaccusative verbs. There has also been the incorporation of lexical loans and, to a lesser extent, grammatical loans. Other phenomena are the *voseo* (the use of *vos* as a second person singular pronoun), uses of gerund, functional loss of the subjunctive, alterations of unstressed pronouns, anomalous uses of the verbs *ser* and *haber*, as well as local peculiarities in the verbal system. All of this indicates that languages evolve slowly enough so that in five hundred years the divergences between varieties are evident in phonetics and lexicon, but

---

8 A grammatical category is "closed" if it does not allow for new words to be created in the same category. These words fulfil a grammatical function and it is impossible to increase their number.

9 A language from a period of Spanish history that extends from the end of the XV century to the end of the 18th Century. This language is characterized, in linguistic terms, by a series of phonetic and grammatical developments that led to the transformation of medieval Spanish into modern Spanish.

less so in syntax, making it difficult to even refer to them as dialects. They are all different ways of speaking the Spanish language.[10]

I will now discuss another example that shows the slowness of linguistic change; this time, we will focus on Spanish. The text of the *Cantar de Mío Cid* (literally "The Song of my Cid"), dating back to the 13th Century, which relates the heroic exploits during the last years in the life of the knight Rodrigo Díaz *el Campeador*, is written in a Romance language, and this is none other than Castilian. It is characterized by the deliberate use of an archaizing language full of neologisms, Latin cultisms and Arabisms[11]. The same happens in Catalan. The language used in the 13th Century by Ramon Llull, the creator of literary Catalan, whose work precedes that of Dante Alighieri in the use of a Romance language, is unmistakably Catalan. There is no doubt either as to what language is used in the *Quatre grans Cròniques* ("Four Great Chronicles") of the Crown of Aragon, the best set of historiography of medieval Europe. The chronicle *Llibre dels feits del rei en Jaume I* [12] (the chronicle of James I, King of Aragon) and the chronicle of Bernat Desclot[13] were written in the 13th Century; the chronicle of Ramon Muntaner[14] and that of Pere III el Cerimoniós,[15] in the 14th Century.

It is surprising that medieval Catalan should be so unitary. From the Pyrenees to Mallorca and Valencia, there is no sign of any dialectal variation. The dialects of Catalan do not offer distant linguistic varieties, only pronunciation differences, appearing during the 16th or the 17th Century. This regularity of the language permeates the literature to such a degree that it achieves an almost perfect uniformity. This is difficult to attribute to the imposition of the

---

10   ALEZA IZQUIERDO, MILAGROS. *Algunos aspectos gramaticales en las modalidades americanas de la lengua española*. AFA-LIX-LX tomo II (2004), pp. 1003-1030.

11   The original text dates back to the second half of the 12th Century, although the oldest manuscript, preserved in the National Library of Spain, is from 1200. The language used is that of a learned author, a lawyer who must have worked for a Chancellery or perhaps as a notary of a nobleman or a monastery, since he knows the legal and administrative language with technical precision, and masters several styles – among them, naturally, the style of the medieval chansons de geste. Main source: Montaner Frutos, Alberto (ed. Lit.), Cantar de mio Cid, Barcelona, Crítica, 2000. Other sources at: http://es.wikipedia.org/wiki/Cantar_de_mio_Cid

12   James I the Conqueror, king of Aragon and Count of Barcelona (1208-1276)

13   Catalan chronicler of the second half of the 13th century, narrator of historical events from the reign of Ramon Berenguer IV to Peter the Great (King Peter III of Aragon, 1240-1285). His chronicle is known as *Llibre del rei Pere d'Aragó e dels seus antecessors passats*.

14   Ramon Muntaner (1265-1336), Knight and chronicler of the Aragonese Crown

15   Pere el Cerimoniós (King Peter IV of Aragon, 1319-1387)

courtly language because, if this were the case, there would always be some testimony of coetaneous speeches seeping into the texts. According to Antoni M. Badia i Margarit,[16] the Catalan dialects have not been constitutive but rather consecutive.

Therefore, we see that the internal sources of changes experienced by languages such as Catalan and Spanish are slow. So slow in fact that more than seven hundred years later we can still fully understand the written language. And both languages are indeed well developed; neither one is a dialect of the other, but from the earliest texts we can appreciate their independency. The two languages have been in contact with each other for seven centuries, not only as neighbouring languages but also due to population movements and the existence of many bilingual families throughout the country. Despite some vocabulary and even syntactic transfer, they continue to maintain their own internal coherence and cohesion; there has been neither blending nor the creation of a linguistic hybrid or interlanguage. Again, we find that changes occur synchronously, i.e. there is a territorial continuity, with transit zones and isoglosses acting as linguistic borders[17].

So, if the Catalan and Castilian Romances are already recognizable and developed in the 12th and 13th Centuries, when were they formed? And what was spoken before them? It was Mozarabic, we are told. But what is Mozarabic? It is a group of Romance languages written in *Aljamía*, i.e. using the Arabic alphabet, or in Ladino if written with the Hebrew alphabet spellings. Sephardi Jews referred to their language as *espanyol* (Spanish). With regard to the writing using Arabic characters found mostly in Andalusian territories, the traditional explanation we are offered is that Latin, which never ceased to be spoken, blended with Arabic. Evidence, however, indicates otherwise. Let us look at an example of an *aljamiado* text:

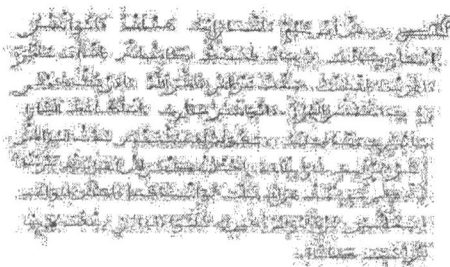

---

16 BADIA I MARGARIT, ANTONI. *Gramàtica històrica catalana*. Editorial Teide 1951 (1994), p. 49.

17 GARGALLO, JE. *Les llengües romàniques. Tot un món lingüístic fet de romanços*. Barcelona: editorial Empúries SA (1994) (Chapter *De fronteres Linguistiques (i administratives; i naturals)*), pp. 175-195.

Externally, it looks like Arabic. But its content is not. An approximate transcript would be:

Dixo un alim [=ulema] d'este rreyno hablando de nuestro encerramiento:
«Yo bien conozco que somos en una temporada de grande espanto, mas no por eso dexara Allah de darnos cautoriçada [=castigo] si dexamos el pro'o [=el pro, la ventaja] de nuestro poderío en lo que toca al preçeptado mandamiento. Y a quanto l'amonestança [=el disimulo, la taqiyya], todos la podemos usar por la bía prebilejiada y con los cantares ajenos por donde los christianos hacen salva, pues todo cabe debaxo de buena disimulança, porque la buena doctrina no la puede bedar ninguna ley por inumana que sea».[18]

The Moriscos were writing in their native language, using the script they considered 'scholarly', which was Arabic, the language of their religion, just as Latin was to Christians. And yet, the transcription of this text shows that this is clearly a Romance language. It is not a blend of Arabic and Latin; it is a Romance language that includes Arabic terms. And this would seem logical if, as we mentioned, Latin was only a written (and not spoken) language.

But what about Arabic? It was a living language! Christians, Muslims and Jews coexisted in Al-Andalus for eight hundred years (711-1492), favouring the exchange of ideas, legends, habits, customs, cultures and religions. During these eight hundred years there were major migratory movements, there was coexistence and confrontation, there were pilgrimages as well as cultural and trade trips. The Arabs remained in the Iberian Peninsula much longer than the Romans. We should be speaking Arabic!

In 711, the first Arabic invasion occurred. Tariq Ibn Ziad was of Berber ethnicity. Although he used Arabic as the language of the chancellery, there were less than 300 Arabs in his army. Then the caliphate was established, followed by the Almoravid conquest and the Taifa kingdoms. Populations

---

18 Example of an aljamiado text by Mancebo de Arevalo. The passage is an invitation to the Moriscos or Spanish crypto-Muslims to continue complying with Islamic requirements despite legal prohibitions and to disguise and protect themselves by publicly showing adherence to the Christian faith. Transcription with an approximate Castilian spelling of that time. Source: http://es.wikipedia.org/wiki/Aljam%C3%ADa

Its resemblance to modern Spanish is so clear that reading and understanding it poses no difficulty for a current speaker

For a better understanding of the Aljamiado-Morisco documentary legacy, please refer to the inventory carried out by Juan Carlos Villaverde Amieva at the Spanish National Library:

http://www.bne.es/es/Micrositios/Exposiciones/MemoriaMoriscos/documentos/estudios_6.pdf

of various origins - Arabs, Berbers, Muladis, Mozarabs, Almohads, Nasrids, Goths and Visigoths - all merged, forming the Andalusian population. So then, why do we not speak Arabic? Perhaps it is because the mere presence of a language is not enough to guarantee its penetration into common speech. Although it is assumed, a deep functional grammatical alteration does not occur; the changes are always confined to the lexicon transfer.

Why is this? What is it that maintains the internal cohesion of grammatical structures over centuries and even millennia? We are clearly overlooking a major aspect!

A team of linguists has developed a linguistic Atlas[19] containing 76 American Creole languages that stem from contact between settlers, indigenous populations and slaves. Much to their surprise, they have noted that grammatical patterns can be traced back to the languages of Africa and the Pacific. How is that possible? Because languages travel with the women!

The grammatical structures of languages have the potential to preserve their characteristics (and those of their ancestors) over very long periods of time. Historical grammar (the comparative method) often makes the 'mistake' of relying on lexical comparatives and therefore the lexicon transfer may create the mirage of a linguistic hybrid. However, in a language, the grammatical patterns (morphology and syntax) remain faithful to only one of the languages in contact. And that is usually the language transmitted from mother to child, not the language of the colonizers!

2.2 The way we think, the way we talk

In order to understand this point, we can reflect on what happens with biological diversity. Species become genetically different in response to geographic separation. For a change to take place in ecosystems, there must be a climate change, a catastrophe or a habitat invasion by destabilizing agents. These are all external causes which produce more or less rapid changes. But they do not create hybrids. Hybrids, like the cross between a mare and a donkey, produce sterile animals such as a mule. So, are languages too subject to the habitat, and do they depend more on the territory than on population changes? The answer is: it depends. For internal changes, the answer is affirmative: there is a lexical, phonetic and semantic continuity related to territorial continuity, and this takes 'time'. For external changes, the answer is negative. We cannot study a language like we would a mushroom

---

19 *Atlas of Pidgin and Creole Language Structures (APiCS).* This Atlas can be viewed online at: http://apics-online.info/

isolated from its habitat. There are universal laws that apply to linguistics just as they do to biological processes.

> Language is much more than a system for communicating. We also use language to think and to organize our own thinking, our inner thoughts. When studying comparative grammar, this aspect is sometimes not taken into account.

To say that speakers lost grammatical cases and that grammatical genders were eliminated is to say that they could not think or make the connections that would allow them to correctly structure abstract cognitive processes! If we take note of how we think, then we should also understand how languages can - or cannot - evolve. Ways of thinking and ways of speaking are intrinsically and indissolubly linked.

In addition, language obeys the laws of physics. Science recognizes that the information about everything that happens to us is stored in our cells. Hence, language too is part of this information and is stored in this way. We do not mean it only at a psychological level. Words said to us when we were young, which caused us an emotional reaction, whether they hurt us or filled us with motivation and affection, all helped us in our development; they are all part of our neurolinguistic programming, and determine the way we see the world.

We receive inputs at different levels (senses, feelings, perceptions and even intuitions). Language is the element that allows the interconnection, exchange and understanding of the information between the internal cognitive processes of the mind and the external context. Knowledge is structured by language. Each language has its own way of structuring this information; and that is transmitted from parents to children, unconsciously, through language. A verb framed language (such as Catalan or Spanish) is not the same as a satellite framed language[20] (such as English). A language that places the verb in the central position (S-V-O) is not the same as another that places it at the end of the sentence (such as Latin). A change in the syntactic order is not a trivial thing: it is much deeper than it may seem because it dismantles the complete puzzle of this self-organizing mechanism, it modifies the hyper-incursion at an epigenetic level. This is why bilingual people increase their cerebral plasticity and improve their capacity for

---

20 Linguistics professor Leonard Talmy, of The State University of New York, is one of the pioneers in the field of cognitive linguistics. Professor Talmy is known for his binary classification of languages into verbal frame and satellite frame languages.

understanding, interrelation and response at all levels. Speaking different languages is an excellent exercise to keep our mind agile and open to new concepts. Language is the characteristic that makes us genuinely human. As Noam Chomsky demonstrated in his generative grammar, we are born genetically prepared to speak![21]

Time and again, we find that certain changes in speech occur more rapidly if there is separation between the groups of speakers. On the other hand, groups that have settled in the same place are inclined to preserve continuity. Languages are conservative and tend to remain unchanged and unalterable over time, despite having contact with neighbouring communities of speakers with which linguistic isoglosses are established. It is like a law that goes beyond phonetic, semantic or structural similarity; beyond the evolution from /P/ to /F/, for example. It is a coding law of inheritable sequences and conceptions that causes certain words to preserve traces of their ancestral origin for millennia, while spoken on the same territory.

What then causes divergence? This is another very interesting question! Divergence itself does not seem to happen randomly.

---

[21] For an in-depth explanation, see JIMÉNEZ HUERTAS, CARME, *Los orígenes del lenguaje* (The origins of language) (2018, in press).

CHAPTER 3

3.1 The non-existent vulgarization process of Latin

Linguists use the term Vulgar Latin in reference to the language spoken by the common people during and after the classical period. *Romanist* linguists use the term to designate the colloquial language of the Lower Empire and of the following centuries until the 'arrival' of the new forms of the Romance dialects. Some linguists prefer to call *Late Latin* the language used from the 4th Century AD onwards.

The hypothesis that separates cultured and Vulgar Latin into two parallel languages is no longer supported by the majority of linguists. Today it is recognized that Classical Latin was a written language that differed significantly from spoken Latin in its pronunciation, vocabulary and grammar. In addition, and as we have seen in the chapter on *What language did the Romans speak?*, it seems that some of these traits appeared very early on.

What was Vulgar Latin like? There is no written record that would directly testify what Vulgar Latin was like. Late Latin was used for writing and differed in style from Classical Latin but was not the spoken language either. Therefore, to describe it, indirect sources as well as the comparative method between different Romance languages are used to identify its differences from Classical Latin. Latin authors cannot be of much help because there is no continuity; the model is always the classics. We must resort to the prescriptive grammars of Late Latin, where the authors condemn the most frequent errors in speech. And finally, the spoken language can be identified with the aid of those texts that show a poor command of the Latin language and use incorrect grammatical forms and structures, as well as texts that contain solecisms, with their syntactic irregularities, and anacoluthons, i.e. inconsistent constructions and expressions that have deviated from Classical Latin.

Therefore, an important lapse of time exists between the last Iberian writings and the earliest writings in Romance, which prevents us from clearly identifying the evolution of spoken language. A slightly more accurate term to describe these vernacular speeches on the Iberian Peninsula would be proto-Romance, or proto-Iberian-Romance.

This period, which begins around the 3rd Century and continues until the 7th-8th Century, has so far been explained through a series of theoretical processes that would justify the formation of the proto-Romance languages through Latin, without considering the elements that could be found in the substrate preceding this presupposed Romanization. The reason is simple: almost nothing was known of the Iberian substrate. Therefore, instead of performing the algebraic operation:

Iberian substrate (I) + Latin and other Italic languages (L) = Proto-Romance (P)

and then reversing the addends to achieve a formula where: P - L = I

one of the elements of the sum was simply omitted, as if it did not exist.

As we have seen, if the mixture must be based on the syntax of one of the two languages, and the result is not similar to Latin, we must assume that it resembles the other element of the addition. However, historical grammar studies have attempted to explain the result as a linguistic evolution or change due to the 'vulgarization' of Latin.

For all the above, there is no empirical evidence demonstrating the existence of Vulgar Latin. Evidence shows that Classical Latin was used for writing and other languages were used for speaking. Whatever the Proto-Iberian-Romance language that supposedly led to Mozarabic was, it must have taken shape after the disintegration of the Roman Empire, between the 3rd and 7th Centuries, based on what is known as Late Latin, i.e. the written representation of Classical Latin plus the influence of contemporary languages.

Before jumping to conclusions, let us examine more closely what happened over the course of those four hundred years that presumably transformed Latin into Vulgar Latin.

3.2 The oldest texts in Romance languages

In the third Council of Tours held in 813, it was decided that the clergy should preach in the vernacular so that the audience could understand them. How is it possible that, in just four hundred years, Latin had grown so far apart that it was incomprehensible? Even today, with a little patience, we can maintain and understand a conversation with an Italian or Portuguese. If you are advised to stop preaching in Latin, there are two obvious reasons:

- Indoctrination through the sermon was important, so it had to be delivered in the language of common people.
- Latin was a language reserved for learned people, clearly incomprehensible to most of the population.

This is so obvious that its meaning is almost overlooked: nobody spoke Vulgar Latin. What did they speak then? This idiom was a Romance language, which we can still understand twelve hundred years later. If it were true that the spoken language stemmed from Latin, it would mean that it was a language separated from its parent tongue only three hundred years before, so it should be more similar to Latin than our present languages. So how can it be explained that people did not understand it? The time elapsed was a quarter of what separates us now from those times.

In the year 842, less than thirty years after the Council of Tours, the Oaths of Strasbourg, which reproduce mutual pledges of allegiance between Charlemagne's heirs, were written in two languages: *Teudisca lingua* and *Romana lingua*. This is the earliest surviving written document in proto-Romance tongues. It is worth reading:

> *Teudisca lingua:*
>
> *In Godes minna ind in thes christianes folches ind unser bedhero gealtnissi, fon thesemo dage frammordes, so fram so mir Got geuuizci indi mahd furgibit, so haldih tesan minan bruodher, soso man mit rehtu sinan bruodher scal, in thiu, thaz er mig sosoma duo; indi mit Ludheren in nohheiniu thing ne gegango, zhe minan uuillon imo ce scadhen uuerhen...*
>
> *Romana lingua:*
>
> *Pro deo amur et pro christian poblo et nostro commun salvament, d'ist di in avant, in quant deus savir et podir me dunat, si salvarai eo cist meon fradre Karlo et in aiudha et in cadhuna cosa, si cum om per dreit son fradra salvar dist, in o quid il mi altresi fazet, et ab Ludher nul plaid nunquam prindrai, qui meon vol cist meon fradre Karle in damno sit.*
>
> **English translation:**
>
> *For the love of God and for Christendom and our common salvation, from this day onwards, as God will give me the wisdom and power, I shall protect this brother of mine Charles, with aid or anything else, as one ought to protect one's brother, so that he may do the same for me, and I shall never knowingly make any covenant with Lothair that would harm this brother of mine Charles.*

The first text is written in a Proto-German language of Frankish type which was spoken in the Rhenish region. We are not in a position to assess the distance that separates it from the present languages. Hence we will focus on the second text, written in Proto-French, a language that was clearly not Latin but neither was it French because it lacked the distinctive features of French that can be found, for instance, in the literary text of the *Canticle of Saint Eulalia*, included in a collection of Latin sermons by Saint Gregory dating from around 880. Strangely, the second text is easy for a Catalan speaker to read: the only foreign element is the position of the verb, in this case displaced to the end of the sentence. So, in fact, this text is more intelligible for a Catalan than for a French speaker!

Although this bilingual text of the Strasbourg Oath is used to demonstrate a contrast between the different speeches and to illustrate its evolution from Vulgar Latin, the evidence itself casts doubt on the claim it wishes to defend: what we can clearly see, in reading this text, is that in 842 there was a perfectly structured language that had little to do with Latin. The fact that the *Romana lingua* of this oath is completely intelligible to a Catalan of today makes one wonder.

The distinctive characteristics of the Romance languages have been studied indirectly, through texts written in Latin. At a very early stage, we find indications of these characteristics that allow us to assert, for example, that Catalan did not come about after the Carolingian Reconquest[22], as it has been said on more than one occasion, but that it originated precisely in the area where it is being spoken today. It is indeed similar to Occitan because they share a common substrate, i.e. they stem from a same parent tongue that was spoken on both sides of the Pyrenees. However, this common substrate cannot have been a Vulgar Latin: this is indicated by the distance we discover between the first proto-Romance speeches and Latin, and by the enormous affinities shared by speeches such as Occitan and Catalan, thus confirming an old relationship between the two cultures prior to Romanization and continued throughout Visigothic and later periods.

In Castilian, the oldest testimonies of the vernacular languages can be found in the *Glosas Emilianenses*, written at the Monastery of San Millán de la Cogolla. They are handwritten annotations, made between lines or in the margins of some passages of the Latin codex *Aemilianensis 60* dating back to the end of the 10th Century or, according to recent studies, more likely to the beginning of the 11th Century. The intention of the scribe monk was probably to clarify the meaning of some of the passages of the Latin text.

---

22   In addition, I recommend the book written by MORAN, JOSEP and RABELLA, JOAN ANTON, *Primers textos de la llengua catalana*, published by Proa (2001).

There are more than a thousand notes, written sometimes in Latin and some other times in a Hispanic Romance (according to current philologists it would be Navarrese-Aragonese in its Riojan variety, although others prefer to call it Castilian with Riojan elements). There are even two notes written in medieval Basque.

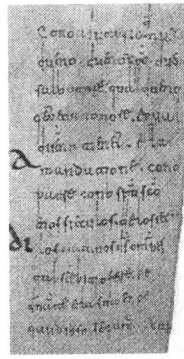

NAVARRO-ARAGONÉS	CASTELLANO	ENGLISH
Con o aiutorio de nuestro dueno Christo, dueno salbatore, qual dueno get ena honore et qual duenno tienet ela mandatione con o patre con o spiritu sancto en os sieculos de lo siecu los. Facanos Deus Omnipotes tal serbitio fere ke denante ela sua face gaudioso segamus. Amen.	Con la ayuda de nuestro Señor Don Cristo Don Salvador, Señor que está en el honor y Señor que tiene el mandato con el Padre con el Espíritu Santo en los siglos de los siglos. Háganos Dios omnipotente hacer tal servicio que delante de su faz gozosos seamos. Amén.	With the help of our Lord Christ, Lord Savior, Lord who is in honor, Lord that has command with the Father, with the Holy Spirit for ever and ever. God Omnipotent, make us do such a service that before His face joyful we are. Amen.

In the following link you can hear them in 'restored pronunciation':

http://commons.wikimedia.org/wiki/File:Glosasemilianenses.ogg

We have to do justice to Manuel Gómez Moreno by mentioning that he was the one who transcribed and compiled these notes in 1911, while he was studying the Mozarabic architecture of the monastery of Suso, and then sent them to Ramón Menéndez Pidal.[23]

The *Cartularies of Valpuesta* (which date back to between 804 and 1200) and the *Nodicia de Kesos* (dating back to between 974 and 980) are other testimonies that reveal some elements of a Spanish pre-Romance showing characteristics of Leonese and Castilian.

Following are some of the Romance traits of the Latin text of the Cartularies[24]:

1. Diphthongisation of short Latin <e> and <o>: *pielle* (PELLE), *fueros* (FOROS);

2. Loss of internal unstressed vowels: *Elcedo* (ELICETUM), *fresno* (FRAXINUM);

3. Voicing of voiceless intervocalic Latin consonants: *Cabezas* (CAPITIA), *montadgo* (MONTATICUM);

---

23 Ramón Menéndez Pidal (1869-1968), Spanish philologist, historian, folklorist and medievalist, was the creator of the Spanish philological school and member of the Royal Spanish Academy (RAE).

24 Source: http://es.wikipedia.org/wiki/Cartularios_de_Valpuesta

4. Development of palatal and sibilant consonants from Latin consonants with yod: *poço* (PUTEO), *Spelio/Spegio* (SPECULUM), *vinga/vineis* (VINEA);

5. Disappearance of the declension system of Latin, in favour of using the accusative for any syntactic function and developing prepositions to mark it;

6. Formation of the Romance plural in <-s>: *sos, sobrinos*;

7. Evolution of the article from the Latin demonstrative ILLE: *Illa Torka*;

8. Verb forms *fiço, dono (donó), es, pertenez, ba, son*; and

9. Order of sentence structures: subject + verb + complements of the verb, to the detriment of the usual final position of the verb in Latin.

The very same Latin texts used to claim the existence of a Vulgar Latin demonstrate that the proto-Romances were spoken long before writing appeared in vernacular languages. What these texts show is not a timely transposition of lexicon but a marked divergence in phonetic characteristics and in basic grammatical structures of the oral language. Based on this hypothesis, we can state that:

1. Medial vowels <e> and <o> in the proto-Romance languages behaved differently than in Latin, as the vowel inventory was different;

2. Alteration, by syncope, of the syllabic structure does not have an open coda but an implosive coda;

3. A generalized voicing process of voiceless stops is present in all Western proto-Romances;

4. There is a generalized process of palatalization in contact with yod: this is one of the most important characteristics because it refers directly to the Iberian substrate;

5. One notes the presence of prepositions, which are non-existent in Latin: this indicates a language with compositional elements far removed from Latin's case system;

6. One notes the addition of <s> as a plural mark, a generalized process in all Western proto-Romances, clearly differentiated from the five Latin declensions with different case endings;

7. The article, which did not exist in Latin, is found in all Romance languages – just like in Greek and in Arabic;

8. The verbs are far removed from the alleged Latin parent tongue, and yet again they do coincide in the different Romance languages; and

9. The grammatical structure, intrinsically related to the self-organizing mechanism that regulates abstract cognitive processes, definitively distances Latin from Romance languages.

We would like to mention a new study by Rosa Bataller Mascarell[25], *El català naixent. Estudi filològic d'un text del segle XI: Jurament de Compareixença*, analysing a legal text of the first third of the 11th Century. It is an institutional text, therefore written in a scholarly style, with significant Romance innovations at all levels: phonetic, morphological, syntactic and lexical. Phonemically, note the loss of the unstressed <e> and the voicing of the final stops. Morphologically, note the disappearance of the neuter gender and the innovative formation of the future and the present subjunctive. The lexicon also picks up non-Latin words that can be considered genuinely Catalan. But it is above all in the syntax where the distance between spoken and written language is most apparent, because the text has abandoned Latin syntax to place the verb in the first or second position in the sentence. This tendency is also verified in the paratactic formation of the subordinate sentences (loss of conjunctions or Latin connectives).

The linguistic characteristics of the *Jurament de Compareixença,* which is supposedly written in Latin, denote that the written language and the oral language are two different things. Given the legal nature of the text, Latin is used in the heading and in the pre-established protocol formulae, whereas the Romance (in this case Catalan) shapes the rest of the text. This is partly due to the fact that there were concepts that did not have a Latin translation but also because of the need for the different parties to understand the terms of the document to be signed. All this allows us to assume that the reality of the spoken Romance language transpires in the 'Latin' language of the scribe.

We will discuss each of the above issues later on.

Romanists date the rise of the proto-Romances back to the 5th Century, after the disintegration of the Western Roman Empire. The evolution of the proto-

---

[25] A philological study of one of the most archaic texts written in Catalan language, the 'Jurament de compareixença' or *Oath of Appearance*. The linguistic features of the text, both Latin and Romance, are analysed. I conclude that the Romanization of the language in this text may already be enough to consider it as one of the first texts written in Catalan.
Memory of the Degree Thesis, online: http://openaccess.uoc.edu/webapps/o2/handle/10609/15381

Romance languages on the same territories as the current Romances would intensify in the 7th and 8th Centuries.

Thus, it is quite easy to understand why the different proto-Romances diverge from Latin. What is not so clear is why the relationship is much closer among the Romances themselves (given they were supposedly moving away from each other) than between these and the Latin language from which they presumably stemmed...

3.3 Similarities between Romance languages

It is very striking that the process of vulgarization from Classical Latin has produced similar results in all Romance languages, even among those that were geographically separated. Spoken Latin was allegedly the same throughout the Roman Empire and, after the fall of the empire, spoken languages moved away from the parent tongue and started a deterioration process because of the multiple inferences with local tongues. How is it then that the resulting languages adopted the same solutions? If there was a vulgarization of the languages, of all the possible changes that could occur by applying a random or haphazard process, it would make sense that different formulas would have been found for grammatical functions, morphological variants, the order of the constituents in a sentence, and so on. And yet this is not so.

Romance languages not only look very similar but have also adopted solutions that have nothing to do with Latin. For instance, all Romance languages have lost their grammatical cases. All but Romanian, where we find a nominative-accusative form opposed to the dative-genitive form.[26] Yet neither German nor Greek lost any cases. Thus, we see that Latin's system of declensions with case endings is more similar to German than to Romance languages. If it were true that the simplification of the declensions responds to a 'natural evolution' of languages, it would then be applied without exception. And yet it is not.

As we will see in the chapter on phonetics, experts establish changes chronologically, in series. We are told that sound changes caused the loss of suffixes that marked grammatical functions. First, the genitive, dative and

---

26 In the Romanian language, nouns apparently preserve two inflected forms that mark the opposition between N-Ac and D-G. However, if we study these formations more closely, we will see that the article (a non-existent grammatical category in Latin), placed after the noun, is what actually shows the inflection. This is very important because it completely changes the explanations regarding the origin, meaning and formation of words (etymology, lexicology, semantics and morphology). We will expand on this topic when we discuss morphosyntax.

ablative ceased to be used. So, why do the English use the Saxon genitive? The order of the constituents also changed, i.e. the adjective was placed after the noun, rather than before. In English, the adjective goes before the noun; again, English is more like Latin than the Romance languages that presumably stemmed from it. Or, the passive system that is so prevalent in Latin is again found in English. And the most difficult aspect is: infinitive sentences are identical in English and Latin; they are formed with a subject in the accusative[27]. There is no such structure in Romance languages: they all opted for the creation of subordinate clauses introduced by a conjunction plus the verb in the subjunctive mode. Is it all accidental?

If it were true that the Romance languages are the result or consequence of the degeneration of Classical into Vulgar Latin, why did they all adopt identical solutions?

Family trees give a standard view of linguistic evolution as a process of *progressive diversification*, excluding any possibility of convergent evolution. However, it is clear that Romance languages do not follow this principle and show multiple instances of convergence. The accepted explanation attributes this exceptional feature to:

- constant borrowings from Latin;
- contacts between the different languages throughout history; and
- processes of political unification and the formation of national languages.

Did these three conditions indeed occur? It is difficult to confirm. Some Romance languages have not been in contact, and neither have they undergone processes of political unification: the political link disappeared precisely during the fall of the Roman Empire, therefore it did not exist in the formation phase of Romance languages. And yet, inexplicably and contrary to what might be presumed, Romanian and Galician-Portuguese, Catalan and the Asturian Bable have all come to converging solutions!

Thus, the Romanization theory relies on a process of diversification that did not occur. The accepted explanation for the formation of Romance languages remains that, over four hundred years, Vulgar Latin speakers moved away from the Latin characteristics. If there is a succession of four generations in a century, it would mean that, for sixteen generations, people would speak

---

[27] In English, *If you want me to help you* follows the structure ME (accusative) TO HELP (infinitive). In Spanish and Romanian, it is translated by a subordinate clause introduced by the conjunction 'que' (that) and the verb in the subjunctive: *Si quieres que te ayude* (If you want that I help you), or a structure verb with a noun clause as the direct object: *Si quieres mi ayuda* (If you want my help).

without understanding one other! They would live in a state of utter anguish from not knowing how to use a conditional verb properly and would be obliged to gesticulate because they lack connectors... It's ridiculous! There is not a single population on earth that does not have a perfect, well-formed language, in the sense of meeting all the needs for human expression and abstraction at the time of use.

We just have to place languages on a map to see that they diverge linguistically as people move away geographically. We see an example of this progressive evolution on the Iberian Peninsula. Thus, Catalan is in an intermediate or transitional situation between French and Spanish. Aranese is so between Catalan and Occitan. The Fabla and other Aragonese dialects are between Catalan and Spanish. The Asturian Bable is between Spanish and Galician. There are linguistic isoglosses that mark well-defined territorial boundaries. Precisely because of this, we are surprised that there are similarities between languages that are not directly in contact: this leaves us with the hypothesis of a common substrate already in place before Romanization. As an example, let us mention some similarities between Asturian[28] and Catalan:

- Phonemes that do not exist in Spanish are shared by Asturian and Catalan: the alveolar affricate [t͡s] as in *otso*, clearly differentiated from the phoneme [t͡ʃ] in *echa*;
- Elisions in vowel contacts: *abrio'l caxón* (in Spanish *abrió el cajón* – (he) opened the drawer);
- Pronunciation in [u] instead of [o] of the masculine endings and the first singular person of the present indicative: *blancu, carru, cantu*[29] (although in Catalan it is written with <o>, it is pronounced [u]); and
- Both languages share many substrate words: *brincar, bruxa, cándanu* (English: jump, witch, lees).

As illustrated in these examples, Romance languages preserve significant bonds which show that they are siblings. They share grammatical components and similar phonetic characteristics, which are even preserved between languages that have not been in direct contact in the last two millennia.

The fact that these similarities are also found among even more distant languages such as Galician, Catalan and Romanian seems to indicate that the

---

28 Reference: http://es.wikipedia.org/wiki/Idioma_asturiano

29 In Castilian: *blanco, carro, canto* (English: *white, cart, song*)

common parent tongue must be much older than Latin and that divergence has been very slow.

Therefore, if it is difficult to explain a similar phonetic behaviour between the Asturian and Catalan languages, separated by the Spanish language that is spoken over eight hundred kilometres, it is even more surprising that Romanian has converged and presents identical tendencies, since both countries are separated by at least five different languages, spread over more than two thousand five hundred kilometres and with several mountain ranges along the way.

Consider the following points:

- In Romanian there are fricative and affricate consonant phonemes and the mid neuter vowel schwa found in Catalan. As we shall see in the chapter on phonetics, these phonemes did not exist in Latin;
- In Romanian there is the vowel elision: [m-am dus] from *mă am dus. In Catalan: [me-nat] the contraction of me n'he anat (in Spanish: me he ido - I have gone);
- In Romanian there is [u] as a grammatical morpheme in the singular masculine (in old Romanian, which tends to disappear at present, although it is preserved in compound words): albu, caru, cântu.[30]

We are told that the Catalan words *cap* (head) and *nas* (nose) come from the Latin CAPUT and NASUM; and yet in Romanian *cap* and *nas* are pronounced and written exactly the same as in Catalan! But it is not just single words that coincide: if a Romanian says *tot s-a pierdut*, a Catalan will understand him without hesitation, because we construct the same phrase: *tot s'ha perdut* (in English, everything is lost)[31]. It is difficult to say that these similarities are due to chance. Furthermore, they have much less in common with the corresponding Latin sentence, OMNIA PERDITA. These resemblances between geographically distant Romance languages are not only found in structural similarities, there are also semantic similarities. For example, we are told that the word *casa* comes from Latin, and it is true that the word exists in Latin, although it means *shack*. Romans called their homes DOMUS, AEDES or TECTUM. And yet in Dalmatian, Italian, Occitan, Portuguese and Romanian, in all Romance languages, *casa* means house. How is it possible

---

30 In modern Romanian: *alb, car, cânt*; in Castilian: *blanco, carro, canto*; in Catalan: *blanc, carro, canto* o *cant* (Eastern Catalan from the Balearic Islands). Examples provided by Mihaela Alda.

31 Example taken from GARGALLO JE, *Les llengües romàniques. Tot un món linguistic fet de romanços*. Barcelona: editorial Empúries SA (1994), p.145.

that a global semantic change occurred? It is more natural, more plausible to assume a common origin prior to Romanization than to try and justify a later evolution from a so-called Vulgar Latin...

Let me add a brief commentary about Euskera (or Basque). Although it is not an Indo-European language, it shares a large component of Latin words. Thich has been explained by the position of the Basque people in the middle of Romanized populations. If, as it would seem, Romanization did not take place because there was a previous common language in the territories of *Romānia* (the so-called land of the Romans), then the lexicon could have been incorporated at a much earlier date or it could even have been part of this common parent tongue. Therefore, with the exception of some neologisms and scholarly words of medieval and modern formation, it would no longer be necessary to etymologically explain the derivation or phonetic changes from Latin (a rapid external change) but rather as a natural evolution (a slow internal change).

Latin is geographically and linguistically halfway between Germanic and Romance languages. Where then did Latin come from?

3.4 Romans or Romanians?

We tend to have such an ethnocentric approach that we try to explain the world from a perspective that disregards or ignores any parallel lines of investigation. For instance, in school we learn the language of the country and a foreign language. In the case of Catalonia, two national languages are taught and a third foreign language that is usually English. However, our immediate neighbours, with whom we share political and cultural borders, speak Portuguese, French and Arabic. Yet we do not study these languages in our schools. This occurs at all levels. Universities tend to be even more closed to external influences, and course contents are transmitted without admitting new knowledge or exchanges. Dissertations must be in line with the academic proposals. Students are only allowed to carry out their own research when doing postgraduate or doctoral studies, although here again we have to put things in perspective because it is difficult to find a Thesis Director willing to address a subject that is not consistent with the knowledge accepted by experts in the field. The outcome of all this is that we have excellent specialists in certain narrower fields but little progress is made in new directions with a more holistic and interdisciplinary approach. The truth is that new discoveries are not incorporated into curricular content. Educational systems are so slow to do so that there is a chasm between reality and the fiction we are being taught.

This situation explains why we Catalans have no knowledge of Basque, why Galicians know nothing about Catalan, why Andalusians do not know Asturian Bable, and so on. We could continue with a long, shameful list of mutual ignorance. Going one step further, this situation also explains why Spaniards know nothing about Romanians. In the classrooms, Romanian is only mentioned to say that it is a Romance language, and the explanation ends here. Reality shows us that Romanian immigrants are quick to integrate within Spain due to two reasons:

- They learn our language with astonishing speed (in a few weeks); and
- ethnically, their factions are indistinguishable among the population, so they go unnoticed.

Who are the Romanians? Why are the words Roman and Romanian so similar? Are they etymologically related?[32] The term *Romānia* [pronounced *Romaa:nia*][33] means 'land of Romans' and in theory, it designated all the territories occupied by the Romans (for example, in the Byzantine Empire). However, it has somehow ended up designating the eastern part of the Empire inhabited by the Dacians. The heroic conquest of Dacia[34] was led by Trajan, a Roman emperor of Hispanic origin but it was Emperor Hadrian (117 AD) who organized the territory by dividing it into two provinces: Dacia Inferior (Lower Dacia) and Dacia Superior (Upper Dacia). A few years later (119 AD), the two provinces were reunited under Roman rule. However, over a century later Emperor Aurelian withdrew the Roman administration (272 AD), leaving the region in the hands of the free Dacians. Then came the Goths, the Huns, the Slavs, the Bulgarians, the Ottoman Turks, the Austro-Hungarians and many other peoples that were not mentioned when we were at school. In Spain, we know almost nothing about this Central European country called Romania, constituted on the territories of the historical Dacia, namely inside and outside of the Carpathian arc, on both sides of the Danube river, and down to the shores of the Black Sea.

How could Trajan, born in Italica,[35] near today's Seville, implant the Latin language among the Dacians so completely that it has managed to overcome

---

32 The Romanian word for Romanian is 'român', but the ancient word is 'rumân', as in Spanish, with the meaning of peasant (information facilitated by Mihaela Alda)

33 Here we have a confusion created by the spelling, which in English can be dispelled via pronunciation: *Romānija* (long open *ā*) was the Byzantine province as attested at 1000 AD, while *R(ə) umejnija* is the modern name of the country we have today. This re-designation has a long story that would need a separate study (Information facilitated by Cristina Brescan).

34 The campaigns known as the Dacian Wars took place in 101-102 and 105-106 AD.

35 Currently *Santiponce*, a town in the province of Seville, Spain.

all these historical vicissitudes? Or at least this is the 'official' version, which is harder and harder to keep afloat.

There are sources claiming that there was a genocide and that Roman troops killed or sold some five hundred thousand of the two million Dacians as slaves —a quarter of the population. These figures are meant to justify why the language of the Dacians would have disappeared, why Latin would have been imposed in record time, and then why it would have deteriorated, incomprehensibly, into Vulgar Latin and then further into Romanian. There is no evidence, however, that the Romans actually led an extermination campaign against the Dacians. Their historically documented interest was mainly linked to the gold mines in Transylvania![36] This is why they went to old Dacia, in search of gold and salt.[37]

Moreover, we must bear in mind that the extent of the Dacian territory conquered by the Romans is very uncertain; during its maximum expansion, it would represent 14 to 26% of the territory, and this occupation only lasted for 165 years. During this period there were dozens of riots from the conquered Dacians, with the help of free Dacian tribes.[38] There was never an established 'Dacian-Roman' society. In contrast to what happened in Spain and other countries under the oppression of the Catholic Church, in later centuries Latin did not prevail as a scholarly language either. So how could we explain that contemporary Romania has such a remarkable linguistic unity throughout its territory? Where are the Romanization factors? They are by far much less apparent than in other countries with Romance languages!

When Emperor Trajan conquered Dacia, he said: "I am going to return to the country of my ancestors".[39] His words are not usually interpreted

---

36   Information provided by Steli Ploscar.

37   Information provided by Dimitru Sonea.

38   A list of all these riots can be found online, in Romanian and English, at: http://istorieveche.ro/2014/01/11/23-de-razboaie-si-rascoale-dacice-intre-106- 271-d-hr/

39   The region where Trajan was born, in the valley of the Guadalquivir, was previously inhabited by the pre-Roman Turdetans that many authors define as the ancient Tartessos. I am including a comment made by Georgeos Diaz-Montexano, writer and researcher: "Trajan's statement has been misunderstood. Obviously he was a descendant of the indigenous people of the region, the Turdetans. When he stated that he would return to the land of his ancestors, he was simply saying that his earliest ancestors came from this region of Dacia, i.e. that the Turdetans (and not the Romans) came from the old Eastern Europe, the region of ancient Dacia. As I have studied all this for more than twenty years, I can say it is consistent with several facts and details:

First of all, the presence, in the region of Dacia and in old Eastern Europe, of abundant toponyms with the Turdo form (Turdo is really the root of turdetanos, because the ending "-tanos" is a suffix of origin or provenance). Turdetania is "the country, nation or region of Turdos" and indeed the capital of Turdetania was mentioned as Turta or Turda.

correctly because they are used to justify that no translators were needed in the post-war negotiations. They understood each other because their tongues were related, not because they had been rapidly Latinized. Nobody voluntarily adopts the language of their enemies, and this can be seen in the rest of the countries that were part of the Roman Empire![40]

Today's Romanian has influences from several languages, but it would be fair to assume that its linguistic foundation comes from Dacian.[41] New historical sources state that Dacian and Latin were related and that both stem from a common language, Thracian. Since groups of Thracians settled on the Italian peninsula, including the Lazio, and the Dacians and the Getae were Thracian tribes who spoke the same language, this would mean that they both have the same origin.

However, we have the testimony of Ovid, the Roman poet who, following a confrontation with Emperor Cesar Augustus, was banished to Tomis[42], on the west coast of the Black Sea, where he spent the rest of his days. Ovid describes the language of the Dacians as 'barbarian' but confesses to having written poems in this language. If the two languages had not been very close, how could he have learned the language so rapidly despite being more than 50 years old when he was exiled to Tomis?[43]

Finally, recent DNA studies show that part of the population in the North of the Italian peninsula was indeed of Thracian origin.[44]

If we have so far questioned the veracity of explanations presenting the Western Romances as stemming from Latin, could the same be true for the

---

Secondly, according to sources consulted by Strabo, through Asclepiades who was living in Turdetania as a teacher of wealthy Turdetan families, Turdetans had their own writing (southern Iberian script, surely), grammar treatises, historical records, laws and poems, that dated back to more than 6000 years. And, as demonstrated, in Dacia there was already a proto-writing at least 1000-2000 years before the Sumerian writing, i.e. a writing that in the times of Strabo already dated to 5000 or even 6000 years earlier (there are still many dating processes to be performed).

40 General Mircea Chelaru: "At different stages, the Roman Empire included more than 67 countries with a total of 270 ethnic communities speaking as many languages and dialects. Palestine was under Roman rule for 800 years. The Greeks, for 400 years, and the same goes for the Egyptians. Not to mention Gauls, Francs and Iberians. Today, none of these nations deny the presence of the Roman civilization /.../ as a state organization of their institutions."
Source: https://www.youtube.com/watch?v=PuncMqoc7W8

41 Information provided by Alex S.H. Abaci

42 The current city of Constanța, Romania

43 Information provided by Mihaela Alda

44 ROXIN, DANIEL. *Spiritul dacic renaște*, Ed. Vidia, Bucharest (2012), pp. 55-61.

Eastern Romances? It will unquestionably be better to ask the Romanians themselves. There is already a Romanian movement trying to raise awareness on why it is more plausible for Latin to come from Romanian rather than Romanian from Latin. We do not have enough knowledge to value this hypothesis, but we will provide some information for you to investigate.

The first reference was found when some details about the secret documents of the Vatican were leaked to the press. Miceal Ledwith, advisor to Pope John Paul II, made the following statements, among many others:

> «Even though Latin is the language of the Catholic Church and obviously the language of the Roman Empire much later, and that it is supposed people don't always know Romanian is a Latin language, a key fact not often remembered is that Romanian, or the ancestor of Romanian, is from where the Latin language came, and not vice-versa. In other words, Romanian is not a Latin language; rather Latin is a Romanian language. So I want to salute those people from the Bucegi Mountains, and around Brasov, Bucharest. You are the ones who have provided a wonderful vehicle of the western culture to the world (Latin language).»[45]

There are other ancient references that point in the same direction and that relate Romanians with Thracians, Dacians and Getae. Greek sources mention that the Dacians were sedentary Getae while the Thracians were nomads. Thus, the first would be established in central Europe and a tribe of the latter would move to Latium and give rise to the Latins. Another reference that we would like to record are the books of Dr Lucian Iosif Cueşdean,[46] who has spent more than twenty years investigating, and discovered that the Getae tribes expanded throughout Europe, even reaching India:

> «Current Punjabi population from north of India is the descendant of a tribe of Getae located in central Asia, over 2500 years ago. These descendants of Getae speak a language close to Romanian. But many of their Punjabi words are also common to Latin. The only problem is that, 2500 years ago, there was no Roman Empire. Which means that Getae did speak a Latin language way before the Roman expansion.»[47]

---

45 Source:http://www.youtube.com/watch?feature=player_embedded&v=Nue1A3PoJrg#! (minute 52:21)

46 http://solif.wordpress.com/oferta-de-carte/

47 http://andreeasoarero.wordpress.com/in-asia-over-80-000-000-people-speak-romanian/

According to Cueșdean, there are currently some 80 million people in the region of Punjab, India, who speak a language similar to Romanian, which allows him to establish that Romanian is older than Latin.[48] The conclusion is that, in ancient times, a single common language was spoken in Europe, related to the Romanian or Dacian spoken by the Getae, which gave rise to the Indo-European languages, including Latin.

Moreover, we must consider the earliest form of writing in the region of the Balkans. The Tartaria tablets, belonging to the Vinča-Turdaș culture, made the dating possible because they were found in an archaeological context next to the bones of a woman. The analyses have dated them to 5300 BC. The tablets contain symbols considered by many researchers as the earliest form of writing in the world.[49] They share signs with scriptures found in Serbia and Bulgaria. Strangely, many of these symbols show a formal similarity with the painted flints found in the cave of Mas d'Azil (Ariège, France), dated to the Mesolithic, or the stones of Alvão (Portugal), dated to around 4000 BC, which remind us of the characters of Tartessian and Southern Iberian scripts. This hypothesis would locate the origins of writing in the West, rather than the East, although this has been systematically dismissed, alluding to the fact that no evidence has been found to demonstrate a complex social organization such as those existing in the Middle East. The reason for this disregard may be due to the modern parameters applied, which do not conform to reality since the earliest examples of writing are neither legal nor administrative texts. As Harring Haarmann[50] rightly defends, in ancient Europe the use of writing was sacred and linked to places of worship.

According to M. Gimbutas, a Lithuanian archaeologist, there was an ancient civilization in Europe that was not Indo-European, which has its roots in the Stone Age. In the 7th millennium BC, various regional, indigenous cultures would have been formed without the influence of Asia Minor, and by no

---

48 His statements about Punjabi need to be corroborated. There are some similarities, i.e. Punjabi verbs have the presumptive mode, which also exists in Romanian (especially in ancient Romanian and in certain modern dialects), although it is no longer studied at school. It also has different forms for masculine and feminine in verbal inflection (for compound tenses), which appears in ancient Romanian and conservative dialects (Mihaela Alda).

49 GIMBUTAS, MARIJA. *Civilizație și cultură.Vestigii preistorice în sud-estul european*, Ed. Meridiane, Bucharest (1989), pp. 65-68 with Figures 5-7, *Civilización y cultura*;

Ditto, *Civilizația Marii Zeițe și sosirea cavalerilor războinici. Originea și dezvoltarea celor mai vechi civilizații europene (circa 7500-700 î.e.n.)*, [in English: The civilization and arrival of the knight warriors of the great goddess. The origin and development of the oldest civilization in Europe (around 7500 to 700 BC)], Ed. Lucrețius, Bucharest (1997), pp. 37-41, 137-143 with Figures 34-54.

50 HAARMANN, HARALD. *Universal history of writing*. Editorial Gredos, Madrid (2001), p.73 et seq.

means would they have fallen behind the contemporary cultures of Asia Minor. In the middle of the 6th millennium, the Vinca-Turdaş culture[51] came to the fore.

This issue still requires some careful research. If it is confirmed, the earliest forms of European language and writing could be from the Balkans.

3.5 Features of Latin

Our discussion so far has positioned Latin chronologically and culturally. I will now describe Latin in linguistic terms.

Latin belongs to the Indo-European group of languages and is related to the following idioms of the Italian Peninsula:

- Italic languages, such as Faliscan, Oscan, Umbrian;
- Celtic dialects, spoken in the north of the Italian peninsula;
- Greek, spoken in the south of the Italian peninsula (Magna Graecia); and
- Etruscan, which is not an Indo-European language but through which it adopts its alphabet (of Greek origin).

Latin maintains affinities with Italic and Celtic dialects, which suggests a common Italic-Celtic coexistence subsequent to the distant separation of the Indo-European trunk.

The characteristics of Latin that separate it from other Indo-European languages are:

Phonetics

- The accent: at first, it had a musical character; later on, it became intensive;
- A trend towards monophthongization;
- The abridging or disappearance of certain unstressed medial vowels: ARIDUS > ARDERE;
- The reduction of stressed diphthongs: OINOS > UNUS, DEICO > DICO;
- The loss of the primitive intervocalic /i, u/: TREIES > TRES;
- The transformation of the initial group /du/ > / b-/: DUENOS > BONUS;

---

51 GIMBUTAS, MARIJA. *Civilizație și cultură*, [in English: *Civilization and Culture*], p. 51 et seq.; Ditto, *Civilizația Marii Zeițe* [in English: *The Civilization of the Great Goddess*], p. 15 et seq.; p. 27 et seq.

- Rhotacism, or the transformation of the intervocalic <s> into <r>, a characteristic documented from the 4th Century BC: ARBOS, ARBORIS ; and
- Confusion of primitive sounds [u] and [b] until they became undistinguishable.

Morphology
- Loss of the dual number;
- Innovations in genitive singular and nominative plural in <o> and <u> stems;
- Adverbs ending in *-ē, -m* and *–iter*;
- Creation of the fifth declension;
- Fusion of consonant stems and *-ĭ* stems;
- Fusion of the primary and secondary personal endings in verbs;
- Loss of athematic conjugations; and
- Fusion, of the ancient aorist and the active and medium perfect into the perfect; and fusion of the conjunctive with the optative.

Syntax
- Use of differentiated cases with the exception of ablative, which reunites the old locative and instrumental cases;
- Creation of the *ablative absolute* construction;
- *Consecutio temporum*, or sequence of tenses between the subordinated clause (using the subjunctive) and its main verb, depending on whether there is a relationship of simultaneity, antecedence or posteriority; and
- Use of indirect style, or *oratio obliqua*.

If Latin is the mother of Romance languages, its daughters should be like the mother and preserve a high percentage of the aforementioned Latin characteristics. And yet what we find is that the daughters resemble each other (and converge, when they should diverge) but do not resemble the mother. So, could we have mistaken the identity of the mother?

How come the parent tongue does not bequeath its daughters morphology, syntax, phonetic laws, structure or the order of the sentence constituents, and how come it loses declensions, deponent verbs... whereas all Romance languages have the same syntax, the same plural formation and use of articles, and have conditional and compound tenses…?

We will discuss this in more detail in the next chapters.

3.6 From Latin to Vulgar Latin; from proto-Romance to the Romances

The problem with assuming that Romance languages come from Latin is that a complex theoretical framework has been woven to support a hypothesis whose veracity has, almost in its entirety, not been demonstrated. It is just a theoretical framework of the hypothetical changes that would have happened diachronically until we arrive at the Romance languages. Nobody thought about comparing the Romances and Latin as equals, that is to say synchronically, as parallel and related languages. Doing so means questioning that their relationship would have been one of filiation.

Following is a summary of the chronologies assigned to the processes of linguistic change from Latin to Vulgar Latin:

- The glottal velar sound of the <h> grapheme was lost, in the 1st Century BC: none of the Romance languages has preserved it;
- Appearance of the first palatals, in the 1st or 2nd Centuries AD: this articulation, unknown in Latin, is found in all Romance languages;
- Process of de-palatalization, in the 5th Century;
- Voicing process, in the 7th Century;
- De-voicing of the voicing occlusive, fricative and affricated consonants in the final position, in the 12th Century; and
- De-affrication process, in the 13th Century.

In the above list I have included only some of the major phonetic changes. Here we should add some of the morphological and syntactic changes that overlap and interrelate. For example, Gallo-Romance languages (French, Occitan and Catalan) show a strong tendency to lose the final vowels in an unstressed position, vowels corresponding precisely to the suffixes indicated by Latin cases. It is said that this was why declensions disappeared: a mysterious phonetic tendency would cause fundamental changes in morphology and syntax, i.e. in all abstract cognitive processes of thought!

For many years it was argued that the cumulative changes were influenced by the Celtic process of lenition[52] that led to a readjustment and modification of the whole system. An increasing number of specialists prefer to just talk about *lenition*, without the *Celtic* adjective, because it has not been possible to prove that this was the cause that linked all these changes together. Nor is it clear that a change that occurred in the 2nd Century BC is linked to another that occurred seven hundred years (namely, some twenty-eight generations) later.

We are not questioning if certain evolutions did or did not occur. Rather, it seems like the argumentative machinery has been forced to prove that the Romances stem from Latin, disregarding any evidence that would facilitate the comprehension (and a different explanation) of these processes. Let us take a look at some examples:

- In the Western Romances 'appear' voiced fricatives <v> and <z>, which do not exist in Latin. This is one of the processes explained through the so-called Celtic lenition. However, in the texts written in Iberian, two distinct fricatives are clearly represented: ↑ and M. It is unknown whether the opposition between the two had a sonority nature corresponding to the voiceless [s] and to the voiced alveolar fricative [z] or if it marked a voiceless palatal articulation of [ʃ] type that some say 'was formed' in the 2nd or 3rd Century BC from a voiceless alveolar sibilant [s] plus the glide yod or the palatal affricate [tʃ]. Whatever the process of formation, it is clear that the influence must be sought in the Iberian tongue because, as we shall see, it has two sibilants and a great distribution of the palatal vowel ᴻ.[53]

- Latin had a reduced inventory of consonants. However, it had many twin consonants, i.e. two identical consecutive consonants that caused a similar phenomenon at consonant level as that of vowel length. In Romance languages, all double consonants are simple, except for:

| LL > [ʎ] | Latin GALLU | Castilian *gallo* | Catalan *gall* | English *rooster* |
| NN > [ɲ] | Latin ANNU | Castilian *año* | Catalan *any* | English *year* |

52 Lenition is the phonetic process of weakening some consonants by loss of articulatory tension.

53 Iberian symbol reproducing the anterior palatal vowel [i]. More information on Iberian writing can be found on the web at http://ibers.cat/index.html (available in Catalan, Spanish and English).

That is, the two alveolar consonants, the nasal <n> and the lateral <l>, are palatalized, displacing the articulation point towards the palate. Another exception occurs with the alveolar rhotic, which remains duplicated:

| RR > [r] | Latin TURRE | Castilian *torre* | Catalan *torre* | English *tower* |

And yet, the transformation from a simple alveolar rhotic [ɾ] to a multiple vibrating [r] has nothing to do with Latin, and even less to do with Vulgar Latin. For again we must refer to Iberian, as its writing shows two differentiated vibrating consonants, in all chronologies and territories, that can be represented by the following characters:

- Finally, an example of morphology: Basque, a non-Indo-European language older than Romanization, has a fixed order of phrase elements (sometimes this order is the opposite to the Spanish order!). The Basque verb agrees not only with the subject but also with the direct and the indirect object, being the central element of the sentence. In addition, Basque is an ergative language and does not show the nominative-accusative opposition of Indo-European languages, because both the direct object of a transitive verb and the subject of an intransitive verb are marked in the same way.

Although the Romances are not strictly ergative languages, certain verbal forms (less and less used today) that have a gender agreement with the direct object are preserved. Semantically, they resemble those classified as non-accusative intransitive verbs (structures where the subject is frequently postponed because it has a theme function)[54] but in these cases the difference is that their syntactic function is a direct object. Let us look at an example in Romanian:

- *Am fost făcut podul* (in English: *I had made the bridge*), with agreement in the masculine; in current Romanian: *Făcusem podul*.
- *Am fost făcută mâncarea* (in English: *I had made a meal*), with agreement in the feminine; in current Romanian: *Făcusem mâncarea*.

---

54 Example: *ha llegado un barco* (a boat has arrived), where *barco* is a postponed subject.

In medieval Catalan, the participle of compound tenses was in agreement with the direct object.[55] These constructions, which are in recession, are still actively used when the direct object is represented by a clitic pronoun in pre-verbal position:

He vist la Núria aquest matí; l'he vista aquest matí.[56]

In Valencian and especially in the Balearic language, concordances are extended to other contexts. For example, Mallorcan allows for concordance in the first person, feminine: *m'he asseguda* (in English: I have sat); in the third person: *na Maria no ha tornada* (in English: Maria has not returned); and even for concordance of number and gender with the auxiliary verb 'to be': *na Maria i na Marta ja son tornades* (in English: Maria and Marta have already returned).[57]

What I would like to point out here is the functional differences expressed by the clitic pronouns, which are very active in Catalan. They are also found in Rossellonese (Northern Catalan) and, to a lesser degree, in French and Italian. Some authors consider it a relic from Vulgar Latin; nevertheless, they could be the remnants of an evolution from an agglutinating language to an inflected one. We will return to this later.

Well into the 21st Century, we still do not have sufficient knowledge to allow us to determine whether the changes attributed to the evolution from Latin to Vulgar Latin might be due to the influence of Iberian or to a parent tongue prior to Romanization and to the processes of individualization of Romance languages. These notes have been made to indicate that the phonetic changes or the fixed order of the phrase constituents may have nothing to do with a loss of unstressed vowels or with a 'vulgarization' due to speakers' lack of linguistic competence. Perhaps it is a characteristic of the evolution from the proto-Romances to the Romances: in this process, Latin would have had an important influence, of course, but considerably less than the significance so far attributed to it. Latin became important once converted (largely post-mortem) into Europe's language of culture and power, as discussed in previous chapters.

---

55 Example: *he escrita una carta*, (I have written a letter) in which the participle is in the feminine.

56 In Spanish, there is no concordance between pronoun and participle: *He visto a Nuria esta mañana; la he visto* (I have seen Nuria this morning; I have seen her).

57 Examples taken from: SOLÀ, JOAN ET AL.: *Gramàtica del català contemporani* vol. I, II, III. Barcelona: Editorial Empúries (2002).

Further, I will discuss the linguistic aspects of these change processes. It will be an introductory analysis, with the aim of expanding it in future work.

3.7 Alphabet

The origin of today's alphabet is attributed to Phoenician, where an ideogram was assigned to each phonetic value of the initial consonant of the word represented. A schematic representation would give rise to letters. This theory contains fair assessments but has proven to be insufficient. One reason is that the Phoenician abjad[58] is consonant and non-alphabetic, because Semitic languages do not need to transcribe vowels. Another reason is that we find older writings. And lastly, the correspondence between phonetic values and formal, external similarities is not always preserved.

According to Gómez Moreno, and quoting Diodorus Siculus, the conception of modern writing has to be located in the second millennium BC. Egyptian hieroglyphs would not evolve directly into Phoenician writing, but first into Sinaitic and Cretan writings, and from there would stem the Cypriot, the Aquemenian semi-syllabary, the archaic Hellenic writings and also the peninsular Iberian writings. This common origin in an earlier period would explain the similarities and formal affinities. These, however, do not necessarily imply a phonetic equivalence, as they are used by different languages.

The different Greek alphabets of the 9th Century BC needed to represent consonantal groups. Since Cypriot and Cretan syllabic writings could not reproduce single consonants and did not distinguish between voiceless and voiced stops, the Greek peoples decomposed the syllable into consonants and vowels, so it was the Greeks who created the alphabet proper.

The Latin alphabet is an adaptation of the western style Greek alphabet via Etruscan and the writings of Italic languages. The differences affect letter shape and use.

Thus, the Greek letters Γ, Δ, Λ, P, Y were substituted for C, D, L, R, V.

Π and Σ were substituted for P and S.

The X started to be pronounced KS instead of KH.

The Greek letters Φ, Ψ, Θ, which were used as numerals, had no phonetic correspondence.

---

58 Abjad is a type of writing with symbols only for the consonant phonemes. There is pure abjad (without any vowels), such as Phoenician, or impure abjad (indicating certain vowels through diacritics), such as Hebrew writing.

In the 2nd Century BC, an aspirated H was added to letters C, T and P through a 'scholarly' imitation of Greek, since Latin did not have the voiceless aspirated occlusive consonants <kh, th, ph>.

In the 1st Century BC, Z was added, which in Latin had no use whatsoever except for writing Greek loans; as well as the Greek Y, without modifying its appearance so as to differentiate V (which in Latin was equivalent to <u, v>) from Y (which was equivalent to <ü>).

The alphabet formed at the end of the Roman republic in the 1st-2nd Century BC was made up of 23 letters, 21 actually from Latin and two more (Y, Z) of Greek influence.

How did this 'influence of the Greek' become generalized in proto-Romances? Was it through Latin or directly from Greek? Indeed, if there was a need to add new spellings it would be because pronunciation in the proto-Romances included sounds that were more similar to Greek than to the phonetic inventory of Latin.

The letter <z> had an affricated sound [ds]. It was written as <z, s> after the 2nd-3rd Century AD. The use of this letter was relatively frequent in words that presented a consonantalization of the palatal vowels <i, e> in any of their positions. That is, it appears in those contexts where a palatalization occurs.

Latin script had three graphemes for the [k] sound: K, C, Q, and yet they were all pronounced as occlusive, not as fricative or affricated. The tendency to use Q before <u>, C in front of <e, i> and K before <a, o> was due to the influence of Etruscan writing habits, as M. Hammarström, a Swedish-Finnish researcher, demonstrated. I cannot but point out that this very distribution is found in our writings, so it could be related to an old inherited syllabic tendency apparent in writings such as Iberian, with a clearly archaizing syllabic structure, which graphically reflects this different form of articulation. I do not believe that this differentiation is a whim because it indicates a different palatalization process. It will be discussed in detail in Chapter 4.2.

The opposition between voiceless or voiced labiodental fricatives [f, v], alveolar [s, z] and palatal [ʃ, ʒ], as in affricates [ts, dz, tʃ, dʒ], non-existent in Latin, is not a trivial issue either, because in our Romance languages this opposition has phonemic value.

There were no assimilations in Latin either, although they were so prevalent in Greek. Nor were there palatal nasals. Thus, in Greek, the gamma before <γ, κ, χ, ξ> is pronounced as a palatal nasal [ɲ]. This post or pre-palatal articulation is present in all Romance languages, with different spellings: Spanish <ñ>, Catalan <ny>, French <gn>, Italian <gn>, Portuguese <nh>.[59]

It is striking that Romance languages have developed these articulations that are not found in their so-called Latin parent tongue from which they presumably derive. We will expand on the subject by talking about phonetics.

---

[59] In Romanian, there is no specific notation for the sound <ɲ>, but the phoneme is frequent in almost all Romanian dialects. In the Transylvania region, for instance, the word *bine* (in English: good) is pronounced <biñe>.

CHAPTER 4

4.1 Phonetics

One of the principles of comparative linguistics is the verification of regular phonetic changes:

> Phonetic changes do not occur randomly, but rather a change that affects a sound in a particular position and phonic context affects all the words with this sound in the same position and context.

The analogy that explains the influence of other forms and other morphological patterns on a particular form or set of forms is an irregular process, less generalized than the phonetic laws, which apply without exception.

Although the phonological inventory is very broad, a language prefers to use certain articulatory positions and a limited phonetic inventory. This is because it favours communicative effectiveness: marked oppositions that are easily identifiable by speakers are preferred.

Babies will learn any language they are in contact with. No language is better or worse, nor more or better adapted to some ethnic groups or societies. And yet this process of language acquisition stops at a very early age, at around three years old. From then on, children adapt their phonetic inventory to that of the mother tongue. Therefore, when striving to learn a second language, the process is much slower and more complicated. This is because a second language will be incorporated from the phonemic boundaries of the sound system of the speaker's native language, which act as perceptual categories that restrict and condition the production and perception of speech sounds responsible for imprinting a 'foreign accent' to the new language.

This law of phonetic changes is universal. Therefore, certain changes are not likely that have occurred only due to the influence of languages in contact. The regularity of processes such as the final de-voicing of occlusives or the voicing of fricatives corresponds to distinctive features of the language itself: these are active processes, which are not only difficult to give up but also appear unconsciously when trying to speak another language. This is why it does not make much sense to say that in a particular century we started speaking in a different way because fricatives appeared, or that we palatalized a consonant due to the influence of a possible Celtic yod...

What is yod? A semivowel of palatal nature which, according to the articulatory context, is equivalent to the vowel <i> or to the consonant <y>. What articulatory change does it produce? Palatalization, i.e. the sound moves the articulation point towards the palate. When did it happen? It is not known, but we do know that it does not come from Latin, because Latin had no yod or palatal consonants. Where is it found? Interestingly, in Iberian.

> If we analyse Iberian writing, we realize that the most common vowel is <i> (Iberian: ᴎ). This vowel is the most stable both synchronically and diachronically, i.e., in all territories and chronologies, from Provence to Alicante and from the 6th Century BC to the 1st Century AD.

The <i> is the most widely distributed vowel. It is surprising that, in absolute terms, it is followed by the <e>, because they are two vowels with little marked opposition: the <i> is a front vowel and <e> is a middle vowel, but both are palatal vowels.

> Could it be then that the palatalization we find in all linguistic changes was not an outside influence but one of the characteristics of Iberian?

It seems more reasonable. This articulation or phonetic feature was simply already here. As a result, the changes followed the mentioned universal laws of phonetics and there would be no contradiction between the theoretical explanations and what really occurred when acquiring the language. This explanatory consistency does not obtain if the hypothesis accepted so far, linking linguistic changes to a possible Celtic influence, is preserved.

Before discussing palatalization in further detail, I would like to make a point. Modern Greek is characterized by a phenomenon known as iotacism or itacism,[60] namely the predominant use of the [i] sound, since the letters <η, υ, ει, οι, υι> are all pronounced as iota.

4.2 Palatalization

Palatalization is a phonetic or phonological phenomenon whereby the point of articulation of a consonant sound moves towards the palate (palato-

---

60 The letter η, eta, is pronounced ita.

alveolar region) due to the presence of a palatal vowel. Palatalization usually includes other processes as assibilation (transformation of a non-sibilant to a sibilant sound), fricatization and affrication. Palatalization occurred in all proto-Romance variants. The only Romance languages that did not experience palatalization were Sardinian and Dalmatian.

The phenomenon of palatalization was verified very early on in the Latin period (2nd Century BC) and increased considerably over the following centuries. The reason for its origin is well known: there is a closure and subsequent consonantalization of palatal vowels that are found as the first element of a hiatus. The consonantalization of the [i] vowel is known as yod and usually represented as <y, j>. It happens when a hiatus becomes a diphthong, i.e., when the vowel [i] becomes the glide [j]. There are indications that from the 4th Century AD, yod affected consonant groups and sounds, triggering at least 50% of the linguistic changes in the Romance languages.

If the articulatory phenomenon occurred at such an early stage, what caused it? How did it happen? When and where did it stem from? And why was it so general? If it were the result of the impoverishment of Latin into Vulgar Latin, chronologies should be lower and transformations, trends and phonetic rules should be so different in the various Romances that they should not converge. However, evidence seems to show Latin as the language that moved away from a generalized palatalization. Thus, interestingly, in some ancient Greek dialects there was also a phenomenon of assibilation that consisted of the transformation of the group -τι (-ti-) into -σι (-si-) in certain contexts. The Mycenaean, Arcadocypriot, Lesbian and Attic Ionic dialectal groups show assibilation; the Beatius, Thesalius, Doric and Pamphilian do not. Thus, in Ionic-Attic the word φέρουσι (carry) appears in some non-assibilating dialects as φέροντι.

I would also like to note that, as Nicole Moutard points out,[61] palatalization in Basque is an expressive and, above all, an affective and hypocoristic phenomenon of great importance. It is used in the semantic field of direct relation, in the names of animals, body parts, colours. There is *tipi* (small) and *txipi* (little); *polit* (nice) and *pollit* (endearing).

There are good reasons to believe that palatalization is related to a change in accent and in the syllabic structure.

---

61 MOUTARD, NICOLE. *Étude phonologique sur les dialectes basques* (1975). It can be consulted online: http://www.bidankoze.net/pdf/1975MOUTARD.pdf

4.3 The syllabic structure

The syllable consists of a consonant onset, a vowel nucleus and a consonant coda, having a structure of two consonant margins and a vowel nucleus (C)V(C). Of these three elements, the only indispensable one is the vowel nucleus.

A closed or locked syllable has a consonant margin after the vowel nucleus: VC. Its sound is implosive. For example, the Spanish word *silbar* is composed of two locked syllables:

onset	nucleus	coda	onset	nucleus	coda
s	i	l	b	a	r

On the contrary, the open or free syllable is the one that does not have any margin after the vocalic syllabic nucleus: CV. It is the preferred structure in languages such as Spanish and French:

word		onset	nucleus	coda	onset	nucleus	coda
vaca	SP	v	a	Ø	c	a	Ø
vache	FRA	v	a	Ø	ch	e	Ø

French has very few consonants in coda position and, although they are written following the rules of orthography, they are not pronounced, except when the syllable has an accent: *il est petit* [il 'ɛ.pə.ti].

Margins may be simple or complex, i.e. they may have one or more consonants. Thus, the Spanish word *tren* (in English: train) has a complex onset margin <tr>, a nucleus <e> and a simple coda margin <n>.

The CV syllabic sequence is easier to articulate than the VC sequence because the presence of internal consonants may lead to more perceptual difficulties. The position of the syllabic coda is the most unstable of the syllable and it is a position that helps with the assimilation, elision or simplification of segments in contact. Assimilation is the most frequent phonological process since we tend to adapt when articulating the segments in contact. It is therefore one of the most frequent causes of linguistic change.

Some consonants in the coda position tend to move and become the onset of the next syllable: for instance, let us have a look at the formation of the plural of the Spanish word *tren > tre#nes*. This does not happen in Catalan, which shows a greater presence of complex codas:

	Word	syllable			syllable		
		onset	nucleus	coda	onset	nucleus	coda
Tren	SP	tr	e	n			
Trenes	SP	tr	e	∅	n	e	s
Tren	CAT	tr	e	n			
Trens	CAT	tr	e	ns			

In French, consonants in a syllable coda position are elided (voiceless pronunciation) if the following word begins with a consonant, and reappear if it begins with a vowel. This phenomenon is known as *liaison* and causes the re-syllabification of the segments to form CV-type onsets. For example, the plural definite article *les* is pronounced [le] but if we say *les amis* it is pronounced [le'za.mi]. This shows a clear preference for open syllables in French.

English, however, is a language whose syllabic boundaries are not clear, since ambisyllabicity exists: it is possible to say either *le#mon* or *lem#on*, which hinders syllabic fragmentation.

Returning to the Romances, there is a universal hierarchy for the formation of the syllabic structure that restricts the distribution of consonants. In the onset position, these go from lowest to highest sonicity (increasing) and in the coda position from highest to lowest sonicity (decreasing). Therefore, the maximum sonicity of the syllable corresponds to the vowel nucleus and decreases towards each margin.

The sonic scale, from highest to lowest, is:

> vowels > semivowels > liquid > nasal > fricative > occlusive[62]

In the onsets, this law applies systematically and is the reason why many occlusive sounds are found in the initial word position, followed by liquid sounds or vowels. With regard to codas, it also applies systematically in Spanish, with the sole exception of the formation of some irregular plurals

---

62 The last four categories in this sequence refer to types of consonants.

of foreign origin not regulated by the RAE,[63] such as *robot* > *robots*. Spanish and French have around 24% of consonants in the coda position, while in English and German the percentage accounts for 60%.

In Catalan and French alike, the syllabification process allows joining segments of continuous words. There is a pronounced post-lexical syllabification[64] that favours onsets and displaces codas to convert them into the onset of the next word. This means that the sonic scale is applied before the universal Maximal Onset Principle. However, Catalan departs from French due to its clear preference for complex locked codas.[65] In the word inner position it can group two consonants, and in the word end position up to three:

V	u (one)	CV	bo (good)	CCV	tro (thunder)
VC	ham (fish hook)	CVC	pam (palm)	CCVC	tram (stretch)
VCC	arc (arch)	CVCC	parc (park)	CCVCC	trams (stretches)
VCCC	erms (barren)	CVCC	text (text)	CCVCCC	bruscs (abrupt)

When forming the plural, this formation of words violates the scale of decreasing sonicity that the coda should show since, by adding the fricative to an occlusive consonant, an increase in sonicity occurs.[66]

In Spanish, this process does not occur at the very end of word because the plural is formed by adding <-es>.[67] The consonant groups occur in the syllable onset and can be found both at the very beginning of the word and at the onset of an inner syllable. We found the following formations:

---

63 The Royal Spanish Academy (RAE) is a cultural institution dedicated to linguistic standardization and to fostering language standardization between or within the various Spanish-speaking territories.

64 Post-lexical syllabification is understood to go beyond the boundaries of a word in continuous speech, so that sound segments are concatenated, causing elision, reduction of consonant groups, simplifications, alteration of sonicity, and modification of syllables.

65 PRIETO, PILAR. *Fonètica i fonologia catalanes*. Universitat Oberta de Catalunya (2001).

66 This phenomenon is still more present in the Mallorcan dialect, which allows word endings in CCC where the final segment is not /s/: for example, *ompl* instead of *omplo* (English: I fill).

67 <-es> is added to the acute words ending in <-á, -í, -ú>, to monosyllables, to polysyllables ending in diphthong or triphtong (with some exceptions) and to all voices ending in consonants <-d, -z, -l, -r, -n, -j>. <-s> is added to the singular of the words ending in an unstressed vowel or in <-é, -ó>. Non-acute polysyllables ending in <-s, -x> do not have a plural morpheme.

CV	tu (you)	CCVC	tres (three)
CVC	ser (to be)	CCV#CV	prólogo (foreword)
CV#CC	sagrado (sacred)	CCV#CCV	triplica (triplicate)
CVC#C	cansado (tired)	CCVC#CV	fluctúa (fluctuates)

In Spanish, the frequency in absolute numbers is CV, CVC, V, CCV, VC, CCVC, VCC, CCVCC. This shows that the consonant groups present a difference between the onset and the coda, since they form complex onsets of two segments (CC) in the first and, very often, in the second syllable, the second element normally being a liquid. A note about Basque: here the most frequent syllabic groups are CV-CVV (59%), CVC-CVVC (21%), V-VV (11%). There are no *muta cum liquida* consonantal groups. The main tendency is the open syllable.

At this point, let us compare the syllabic structure of classical Latin with that of our Romance languages, especially with regard to the behaviour of consonant groups known as *muta cum liquida* – that is, any of the occlusive <p, t, k, b, d, g> followed by a liquid <l, r>, which is the onset formation allowed by the laws of sonicity, as mentioned before. What is interesting in this case is that the proto-Romances tend to modify the boundary between syllables, placing the consonant before the liquid in coda position. In the case of the consonant being positioned at the very beginning, an epenthetic vowel is added and the syllable is separated after the liquid:

Classic Latin	Proto-Romances
vowel # consonant + liquid V#CL	VC#L
liquid + consonant + vowel LCV	VL#CV

This phenomenon that eliminates the *muta cum liquida* has its origin in Iberian and is so genuinely ours that it has left marks in the formation of the syllabic structure determining our prosody.

As mentioned while explaining palatalization, when a consonant is in an implosive position (locked syllable coda) and the next syllable begins with a palatal vowel <i, e> or with a palatal consonant, the syllable coda consonant tends to become part of the onset of the next syllable. The vocal tract, which prepares to articulate the new syllable according to the palatal nucleus of a syllable, moves the tongue towards a point of articulation located on the palate. This is the underlying reason in most processes of linguistic change, leading to different solutions for Catalan and Spanish.

In Latin, implosive consonant codas showed very little variety, with a very restrictive distribution, similar to that of Spanish. However, in Catalan and Occitan, consonant codas become complicated and the syllable should not be considered the primary unit. In prosody, an alternation of stressed syllables is equally as important as the phonotactic segments that produce the internal rhythm of this epiphenomenon.

The sound patterns of a language constitute one of its most important characteristics. They are present from the very first months of life and mark a child's acquisition of the language, because his linguistic perception will be modulated, from the time he starts to babble, by the phonology of his mother tongue and of any languages present in his environment. Hence, syllable structure is one of the patterns acquired at a very early age, and is part of the intuitive knowledge of all native speakers of a language.

4.4 The accent

Prosody, or vibration, is the music of a language. It is so genuine that we can even recognize a language when we cannot speak or understand it. By simply listening, we are able to distinguish the intonation patterns of English, Italian or Russian: in each case, we recognize 'its music'.

The prosody and internal rhythm of a language are underlined by the alternation between stressed and unstressed syllables. Since in Romance languages the vowels do not show opposition of duration, the syllabic nucleus and the tonic accent fall on the vowel, so the rhythm fluctuation is marked by the vowel accents.

The stress is a lexical property of morphemes. It is not something that can be changed easily because it is associated with a phonemic value. The different position of the stress can mark semantic and morphological differences, such as verb tenses: *canto* (song, noun; and sing, verbal form) and *cantó* (sang); *término* (term, end), *termino* (finish) and *terminó* (finished), and even differentiate words that have no etymological relationship: *entre* (between, preposition) and *entré* (I entered, verb).

In the words of proto-Romance languages, the stress distribution can have different voices: oxytone (where the stressed syllable is the last one), paroxytone (where the stressed syllable is the penultimate), and proparoxytone or superproparoxytone (where the stressed syllable is the antepenultimate or the previous one). This stress pattern of the Romances coincides with that of Greek and diverges with respect to Latin. The fact that there were no oxytones in Latin distances Latin prosody from the rest of the languages that supposedly derive from it.

Latin accentuation had the following pattern:[68]

syllables	duration of penultimate vowel	nature of penultimate vowel	stress
2	-	-	paroxytone
+2	long	-	paroxytone
+2	short	locked	paroxytone
+2	short	open	proparoxytone

There is another factor that must be considered when talking about stress pattern. In the process of creating new words through composition, there is no vowel reduction or alteration of the stress distribution. Stressed prefixes and suffixes show that, at some level of phonological derivation, there is an internal blocking stress that makes certain compositional units unmodifiable.

Moreover, recent studies show that consonant codas also mark an intra-syllabic rhythm, because although they are shorter than the consonants located in the syllabic onset, in this position and phonic context they increase their sonicity.

4.5 Vocalism

Latin had exactly three vowels <a, o, e> and two semivowels <i, u>. The distinctive feature of vowel timbre was quantity, so the total vowel inventory was ten vowels ā, ē, ī, ō, ū, ă, ĕ, ĭ, ŏ, ŭ.[69] The disappearance of quantity, replaced by intensity, displaced the main stress and caused the weakening of internal unstressed vowels, which altered their vowel timbre.

Historical grammar locates the substitution of quantity for intensity in the 1st Century AD. Nowadays, these vowel changes show different equivalences in Catalan and Spanish. In Catalan, the Latin quantity distinction corresponds to the difference in timbre. Thus, in Latin, long vowels ā, ē, ī, ō, ū would correspond to closed vowels a̧, ȩ, i̧, o̧, u̧; and short vowels ă, ĕ, ĭ, ŏ, ŭ to open vowels a̦, e̦, i̦, o̦, u̦. However, we have no written record showing the existence of five open vowels – but only two: [ɛ] and [ɔ]. The current Catalan vowel inventory contains seven stressed vowels: [a], [ɛ], [e], [i], [ɔ], [o], [u], with eight vowels in Balearic (adding a stressed [ə]).

---

68 MARTÍ I CASTELL, JOAN. *Gramàtica històrica catalana II*. Universitat Oberta de Catalunya (1990).

69 They are distinguished graphically: ā (long vowel) and ă (short vowel).

This inventory of seven stressed vowels could have coincided with that of ancient Basque. Although little is known about the ancient Basque phonological system, R. Menéndez Pidal acknowledges the presence of open vowels [ɛ] and [ɔ] in place names. Furthermore, the fact that there are difficulties in the timbre delimitation between [e] and [i] and between [o] and [u] shows that Basque has different degrees of opening and closing in vowels, i.e. they are pronounced more open and less stressed than in Spanish, showing greater variability. In any case, a vocalism of seven vowels seems to have more affinity with Greek than with Latin or even with Cypriot (which does not distinguish between long and short vowels either).

In Catalan, in an unstressed position a vowel reduction occurs; there are only three unstressed vowels ([ə], [i], [u]) and therefore the stressed and unstressed position determine the vowel timbre. This does not occur in the same way in all dialects. In general, we can say that the three vowels [a], [ɛ], [e] are reduced to [ə], and the three velar vowels [ɔ], [o], [u] are reduced to [u]. The only vowel that is not altered at all is [i]. This information must be important because, as we have explained when speaking of palatalization, [i] is the most common vowel in Iberian and is behind most linguistic changes.

In Spanish there are five vowels with no change of timbre, because currently the onset has no phonemic value.[70]

This feature of short Latin vowels corresponding to the open vowel is not found solely in Catalan. We also find it in Romanian and Galician-Portuguese:

| Latin FŎCUM (fire) | Catalan f[ɔ]c | Romanian f[ɔ]c |

Let us look at another example, on the Latin word FĔRRUM:

| Latin FĔRRUM (iron) | Catalan f[ɛ]rro | Portuguese f[ɛ]rro |

In both Catalan and Galician, the pronunciation is [ˈfɛru]. In fact, Catalan and Galician-Portuguese opted for an inventory of open and closed stressed vowels: both languages show a clear tendency to close the unstressed [o], which changes to [u]. Historical grammar states that the confusion between graphemes <o, u> began in the 15th-16th Century, according to when it has been found in writing. However, how is this late chronology explained if

---

70 The vocalism of old Castilian could have been different from today's, which is composed by an inventory of five vowels: a, e, i, o, u. Its percent distribution corresponds to that of Basque. It is not singular; the absence of <f-> in the initial position *(harina, hierro)* is also a feature shared with Basque. There is a significant gap from medieval Castilian to modern Spanish, which took place between the 15th and 18th Centuries. If we analyse the language of Gonzalo de Berceo and the chansons de geste, such as *El Cantar de mio Cid*, we find many similarities between the language spoken in Castile and other Romances such as Galician, Romanian and Catalan.

the language of formation is supposed to be Vulgar Latin? Hence, why do Romance languages coincide? In Catalan, the usual graphical confusions in manuscripts show that the unstressed vowels <a> and <e> were already mixed up in the 12th or 13th Century, when they appeared before the main stress. Linguists often call these alternations a 'vowel instability', when it is really a completely stable phonetic feature, drawing attention to a certain generalized feature of speech.

In the very last position, confusions are less frequent and solutions differ from some to others. In Catalan, Occitan and French, the final unstressed vowels disappear. In contrast, Spanish, Italian and Galician-Portuguese retain the majority of late unstressed vowels.

We are told it was Vulgar Latin that, from the substitution of the melodic accent for the intensity accent, created the vocalism of the Western Romances. Again, we should wonder how it is possible that languages that have hardly ever been in direct contact have reached identical solutions. If from this premise it is difficult to understand the similarities between Catalan and Galician, it is even more difficult to justify that both languages converge with Romanian. On the other hand, if the substitution of quantity for intensity occurred at such an early period, the answer could come from Iberian: what would happen if we found a vowel inconsistency that demonstrated the existence of vowel alternation in Iberian texts? For it seems that there might be signs of such inconsistency in the middle vowels <e, o>.[71] It remains to be studied if this was an onset or length feature. An inventory of seven vowels would also coincide with Greek, whose epsilon and omicron have their long doubles eta and omega.

4.6 Diphthongs and hiatuses

Ancient literary Latin had five diphthongs: OU, OI, EI, AI, AU. Classical Latin, however, had a strong tendency to monophthongation, i.e. a phonetic change that consists in the reduction of a diphthong to a single vowel. There were only three diphthongs: AU, AE, OE. On the contrary, the tendency of Western Romance languages was diphthongation of the short vowels <e, o> which in Spanish become <ie, ue>, respectively. This phenomenon could be subsequent to Romanization because, in Basque, short Latin vowels do not form diphthongs, like in Spanish. In Catalan, as we have seen, short vowels are equivalent to open vowels:

---

71 ORDUÑA AZNAR, EDUARDO. *Vocalismo átono en ibérico y romance* (2014).

Latin TĚRRAM (earth, land)	Catalan t[ɛ]rra	Spanish tierra
Latin PŎPULUM (people)	Catalan p[ɔ]ble	Spanish pueblo

It is usually accepted that, in most Romance languages, the Latin diphthong AU became <o>. The exception to this rule is found in Galician-Portuguese, where it became <ou> or <oi>; as well as in Occitan and in Basque, where it has remained as <au>. Some examples are:

Latin CAUSA (cause)	Spanish cosa	Portuguese coisa	Occitan causa
Latin AURUM (gold)	Spanish oro	Portuguese ouro	Occitan aur
Latin TAURUS (bull)	Spanish toro	Portuguese touro	Occitan brau

Literary Romanian has many more diphthongs than the dialects. Here are some examples: fier - fɛr (iron; Catalan: *ferro*, Spanish: *hierro*), moara - mɔra (mill; Catalan: *mola*, Spanish: *molino*); câine – câñe (dog; Catalan: *ca* or *gos*, Spanish: *can* or *perro*).

A hiatus is the concurrence of two or three vowels that do not form a diphthong, i.e. they are vowels that belong to different syllables. The phenomenon can also occur between the end of a word and the beginning of the next. Vowels that are in an unstable position tend to contract or diphthongize.

If the first element is a velar vowel <o, u> in an unstressed position, it is often reduced to the point of being suppressed.

If the first element is a palatal vowel <e, i> in an unstressed position, it tends to close and then to group syllabically and become a consonant:

Latin VI-NE-A (vineyard)	Spanish viña	Catalan vinya
Latin FI-LI-AM (daughter)	Spanish hija	Catalan filla

In the first example, both languages share the phenomenon of palatalization of nasal consonant <n>, which, by influence of the vowel context, articulates in a palatal way; only graphemes change. In the second example, there is also a phenomenon of palatalization, of the lateral <l>, but the results show considerable differences: while in Catalan the initial <f> is maintained and the lateral is palatalized in [ʎ], in Spanish there is no initial fricative <f> and the lateral is pronounced as velar, i.e. it moves backwards and articulates as [χ].

Again, we are faced with the phenomenon of palatalization. In the proto-Romances, the Latin vowel <i> is a semivowel or glide, a yod, which is always behind the main processes of linguistic change. This sound did not exist in

Latin. In the previous examples, we can see that the articulatory change alters the syllabic distribution. It also modifies the vocalism, causing simplification of the unstressed vowels of a hiatus, or inflection of the stressed vowels, thus reducing the degree of opening of accented vowels:

[ɛ] > [i]	Latin PECTU (chest)	Catalan *pit*	Spanish *pecho*
[ɔ] > [u]	Latin OCVLV (eye)	Catalan *ull*	Spanish *ojo*
[a] > [e]	Latin FACTU (fact)	Catalan *fet*	Spanish *hecho*

The phenomenon of inflection can even close stressed vowels by two degrees. Historical grammar has not been able to determine the stages of this evolution; it can only figure them out because some conservative Catalan dialects such as *Pallarès* or *Ribagorçà* keep the vowels much more open.

Yod also alters consonantism, creating palatal consonants non-existent in Latin, as I will discuss next.

4.7 Consonantism

Consonantism in Latin was much more reduced than in Romance languages. Latin only had 14 consonants, compared to 19 in Spanish and 23 in Catalan. These consonants were distributed in three orders only: labial, dento-alveolar and velar.

Historical grammar has studied the phenomena of inflection, assimilation, dissimilation, suppression and addition of vowel sounds; and the voicing, devoicing, fricatization and palatalization of consonant sounds of Romance languages in relation to Latin; trying to describe all these processes. The differences in the phonetic inventory are so great that it has been necessary to explain them through complicated evolutionary relationships.

If we focus on the Western Romances, evolution is encompassed in a process of lenition divided into several phases:

1. The earliest would be the simplification of the Latin geminated consonants, all of which are reduced, with the exception of LL, NN and RR, as already mentioned.

    It should be added that consonants' gemination in Latin had a phonemic value, so ĀNNVS (year) did not mean the same as ĀNVS (elderly).

2. This is followed by a process of voicing the voiceless fricatives and occlusives formed from the simplification of Latin geminate consonants.

This is a difficult point to understand. The official explanation maintains that, in order to distinguish the occlusives and fricatives that had been formed from the simplification described in the first point, voiceless fricatives and occlusives become voiced. The compelling question is: why would speakers want to distinguish them? Would they not all be the same to them? That is what should happen, because the first law of phonetics, which we have already outlined, indicates that a change affecting a sound in a certain position and phonic context affects all the words that have this sound in the same position and context. Of course, this is a theoretical argument, rendered vulnerable by being somewhat speculative. Another explanation may be preferred here: the high presence of geminate consonants in Latin indicates that consonantism must have presented a phenomenon similar to the duration of vocalism. The tendency of Latin to show an opposition of duration between simple and double consonants would be equivalent to the short-long vowel opposition. Therefore, the duration feature of Latin corresponds again to a different degree of intensity (onset) in the Romances, equivalent to that found in vowels — which, in consonantism, means that voiceless consonants become voiced. In both cases, changes are in timbre, not in duration!

3. The next phase is approximation of voiced stops.

   What does this mean? If geminate stops have been simplified and the simple voiceless ones are voiced (to distinguish them from those that were already simple), it turns out that voiced stops are now articulated as approximants. Why? Here again the opposition is in voicing and must have an older origin, because it does not make much sense to apply the law of phonetics to some articulations (supposedly to Latin words) while leaving the rest unchanged. What is happening here? There is an attempt to 'force' the phonetic features of the Romances to stem from Latin. But the whole articulatory system is different, because they are different languages. This process of lenition only occurs in Western Romance languages, which suggests that these languages must have evolved from a parent tongue related to Iberian.

4. The fourth phase describes the disappearance of some approximants, according to their position, due to a tendency to become weaker.

5. The next stage involves the voicing of the affricate [ts], an unvoiced intervocalic that becomes voiced [dʒ]. Since this sound was unstable, it became de-affricated, transforming into the voiced alveolar sibilant [z]. Voiceless and voiced stops followed by <r>, called *muta cum liquida,* were

also altered – and they all became voiced inter-vocalically, forming the groups BR, DR, GR.

[PR] > [BR]	Latin CAPRA (goat)	Spanish *cabra*
[TR] > [DR]	Latin PETRA (stone)	Spanish *piedra*
[CR] > [GR]	Latin SOGRA (mother in law)	Spanish *suegra*

Hence, if approximants occurred after the third step, by applying the same 'lenition law' understood as a process of linked changes speakers would have been unable to distinguish the new approximants coming from voiced stops (the same stops that were voiced to be distinguished from the unvoiced stops that had to be distinguished from Latin geminate consonants). Well that's just it, after all these changes, speakers found that the approximants were weakened and disappeared! The formation phase of the voiced alveolar sibilant sound is the culmination of this extremely long process, and this causes the entire system to collapse like a house of cards. Because where did this [z] come from? The last letter of our alphabet did not exist in Latin; it had to be copied from the Greeks and added to its reduced consonant inventory. Where did it come from? It must have been already here! In Iberian! As we already mentioned, each and every Iberian text in all chronologies and territories from the 6th Century BC clearly distinguished two sibilant fricatives. Since Iberian experts do not know if the two sounds were opposed by sonority (e.g. a voiceless [s] and a voiced [z]) or by distribution (e.g. an alveolar [s] and a palatal [ʃ]), they are usually represented as <s> and <ś>.

Another phenomenon was betacism, where, for example, the Latin V is confused with <b>, as it also happens in Basque. In Catalan, the opposition <b, v> is maintained in some areas but is in sharp decline.

At this point, it is easy to understand why the subject of Historical Grammar is a tough nut to crack when studying philology. Nobody understands it. It is clear, however, that the explanations discussed here contradict the principles of sound change. They are only theoretical arguments that have little or nothing to do with the way modern languages behave. Since the mid-19th Century, the Neogrammarian School established a set of universal principles showing tendencies that are met in all languages worldwide, with very few exceptions:

- **Phonetic change has no memory.** It is not possible that a voicing process of voiceless fricatives and stops occurred to distinguish between articulations coming from Latin geminated consonants and those deriving from simple stops. The process of phonetic change only takes into account the current state of a word and does not distinguish its origin. Therefore, any explanation that justifies a lenition process of linking changes that would have occurred over hundreds of years is simply not plausible.
- **Linguistic change is blind to grammar.** Therefore, it takes into account the articulatory context and ignores the meaning of the words. Nor does it distinguish between grammatical categories. Although there are some exceptions by analogy, as a rule phonological change is applied regardless of whether the word is an adjective or a verb.
- **Phonetic change is regular, inexorably applied and does not allow exceptions.**

Although sociolinguistic factors can favour gradual phonetic changes, the universal principles provided above dismantle, as discussed, all the explanations given by historical grammar to demonstrate the formation of the Romances from Latin.

It seems clear to us that a revision of all evolutionary historical grammar is required, which should take into account the following points:

- If we started from a premise of kinship (and not of filiation) between Latin and Romance languages, we would be able to explain these phonological phenomena as part of the phonotactic[72] features of each language.
- It would be advisable to consider alternatives answers, different from the ones officially accepted. If these new answers cover aspects that the previous scientific theories could not explain, it would be good to open up to them.

Let us briefly analyse the differences between the Romances and Latin, by separating the consonants according to their articulation and by organising them according to their sonicity,[73] starting with the least sounding consonant

---

72 Phonotactics is the part of phonology that studies permissible phonetic combinations in a language. It defines combinations, syllabic structures, consonant groups and specific vowel sequences, as well as constraints.

73 We use the term *sonicity* for the perceptiveness of the different sounds grouped in an articulation mode. In the same way and at the same point of articulation, we use the term *sonority* to mark the opposition between voiceless and voiced characters.

(occlusive, fricative, affricated) and continuing with the most sounding consonant (nasal, lateral and vibrant). In each manner of articulation, they are analysed according to the place of articulation, from front to back, and from voiceless to voiced.

To hear the articulation of each phoneme and its displacement according to the manner and place of articulation, I recommend the following page from the University of Iowa:

http://www.uiowa.edu/~acadtech/phonetics/spanish/frameset.html

4.8 Stops (Occlusives)

In initial position, labial, dental and velar stops coincide with those present in Latin.

In medial position, they show different tendencies.

- Intervocalic voiceless stops become voiced:

P > B	Latin CAPILLUM (hair)	Spanish *cabello*	Catalan *cabell*
T > D	Latin RUOTA (wheel)	Spanish *rueda*	Catalan *roda*
C > K	Latin SPICA (sprig)	Spanish *espiga*	Catalan *espiga*

- Intervocalic voiced stops are preserved with a fricative pronunciation:

| B > V | Latin HABERE (to have) | Spanish *haber* | Catalan *haver* |

- In other contexts, medial stops disappear:

| D > ð / Ø | Latin NIDUM (nest) | Spanish *nido* | Catalan *niu* |
| T > D | Latin MAGISTER (teacher) | Spanish *maestro* | Catalan *mestre* |

In contrast, stops in final position or in syllable coda weaken or disappear in most Romances. In Spanish there are few stops in word final position. The treatment of the final stop is different according to the speeches in each territory. Thus, a word such as *salud* (Spanish for health) can be pronounced:

- with devoicing: salu[t]
- as an approximant: salu[ð]
- with fricative realization: salu[Θ]
- with an aspirated h: salu [h]
- with total elimination of the segment: salú[Ø]

Spanish and Greek coincide in their preference for a word ending in a vowel or in consonants <n, r, s>. However, Catalan favours word endings in occlusive and in an occlusive plus a liquid. Regardless of whether they preserve the orthography or alter their writing, all stops in final position have a voiceless pronunciation:

In Catalan:

B > P	*adob* (English *marinade*) is pronounced [əðop], but changes to *adobar*
D > T	*verd* (English *green*) is pronounced [bɛɾt], but changes to *verda* ['bɛɾðə]
G > C	*groc* (English *yellow*) is pronounced [grɔk], but changes to *groga* ['grɔyə]

A note about Basque: at the end of the word there are no voiced stops, only voiceless ones: <-t>, <-tt> and <-k>. And they are plentiful, more than in Catalan, because they are case-based, verbal suffixes and morphemes.

One of the characteristics of Iberian is the apparent confusion between voiceless and voiced stops. Could this apparent inconsistency correspond to a different position and phonic context? If so, this would mean that speakers did not mistake or try to guess them but simply wrote them as they sounded according to the articulatory context. It is a fact to be considered because it is being found in the Cretan syllabic script, in some dialects of old Greek and in other related Indo-European languages.

4.9 Fricatives

The voiceless labiodental fricative [f] is identified with the sound of the aspirated labial Greek <φ> and it used to be transcribed as <ph>. It was not very common in Latin in initial position; in medial position, it was found only in compounds. Its origin is a slightly aspirated fricative sound that we also find in Spanish, and this is the reason why, in initial position, the letter <f> becomes <h>, although in old documents we graphically find the doublet <f, h>. The absence of an initial <f> is considered a feature of Basque, because Gascon also has it. In the rest of the Romances, the voiceless labiodental fricative is maintained.

The voiced labiodental fricative [v] presents two distinct interferences. In Latin, it was confused with [u]. On the contrary, in Romance languages the tendency was to pronounce it just like the voiced bilabial [b]. Although the opposition <b-v> remains in some Catalan speeches, it is in clear decline.

The voiceless alveolar fricative [s] has remained stable in all Romances, both in initial position as well as in medial and final position. In the Western Romances, in final position it becomes the plural mark. In some contexts, before the palatal vowels <e, i> there is a palatalization that is attributed to the influence of the Arabic adstratum:

| Latin SYRINGA (syringe) | French *seringue* | Catalan *xeringa* | Spanish *jeringa* |

While the voiced alveolar fricative [z] did not exist in Latin, in Catalan it has an important phonemic value. In Spanish, the sibilant <s> is pronounced [z] when followed by a voiced consonant and [s] if followed by a voiceless consonant. The Spanish letter <z> is pronounced as a voiced dental fricative [Θ]. The voiced alveolar fricative also exists in Romanian, which again confirms that this phoneme must necessarily be prior to the Romanization process.

In Catalan there are two palatal fricatives, a voiceless [ʃ] in *xarop* (syrup) and a voiced [ʒ] in *jardí* (garden). These sounds also exist in Romanian. Although, strictly speaking, there is no voiced fricative in Spanish, in some speeches we find this articulation in words such as *mayo* (May), which is usually articulated in an approximant way. The pronunciation of the Spanish <j> is an articulated either dorso-palatal [j̰] or velar-uvular, which changing from [x] to [χ], according to the different speeches.

A note on Basque: it has the same sibilant sounds as Catalan, composed of six phonemes and six allophones. This rich range of sibilants constitutes the great difference between Basque and Spanish. How is that explained? We have no answer, so here is evidence to consider:

SIBILANTS	dorsal-alveolar		apical-alveolar		pre-dorsal-palatal	
FRICATIVES	s <z>	allophone z	ś <s>	allophone ź	ʃ <x>	allophone ʒ
AFFRICATES	ts <tz>	allophone dz	tś <ts>	allophone dź	tʃ <tx>	allophone dʒ

Latin had a single voiceless alveolar sibilant <s>. Let us remember that, in Iberian texts, two clearly distinct sibilant fricatives are represented. We still do not know whether the other phonemes existed or not in Iberian. The inventory of sounds of the Iberian language is not yet defined. In fact, if we apply the laws of Grimm and Verner,[74] we should try to identify the affricated and palatal sounds that did not exist in Latin but are found in some of today's peninsular languages.

If Romance languages were derived from Latin, the formation of all these sibilants would contradict the application of the Economy Principle in linguistic change. So, where does this rich phonetic inventory of the Romances come from? Again, the answer points to an earlier parent tongue.

4.10 Affricates

In Catalan there are four affricates, two alveolar [ts] and [dz] and two palatal [tʃ] and [dʒ]. The palatal affricates also exist in Spanish, although they have no phonemic value. These sounds are represented differently, according to the orthographic rules, depending on the context: in Catalan, the voiceless affricate at the very beginning or in the middle of a word is written <tx>, while at the end of a word it is <ig>. In Spanish, it is usually represented by <ch>. The voiced affricate in Catalan is represented by <tg, tj>, depending on the vowel that follows. Thus we have *metge* (doctor) but also *platja* (beach). In Spanish, at the very beginning of a word it can be written with <y> (as in the pronoun *yo* – engl. I), or even with <h> (as in the word *hierro* – engl. iron).

Basque has three affricates, represented as <ts, tz, tx>, which are grouped as sibilants. They have, therefore, been discussed in the section on fricatives.

Affricate sounds did not exist in Latin.

---

[74] The laws of Grimm and Verner – named after Jacob Grimm (1785-1863) and Karl Verner (1946-1896) – are a series of phonetic laws that study the phonetic distribution between the phonemes of the languages and describe the historical evolution of linguistic changes.

4.11 Sonorants

Sonorants <l, m, n, r>, being the ones that 'sound' the most, are usually the most stable. They coincide in most Romances, and also with Latin. Therefore, I will only highlight the differences.

The Latin lateral <l> in initial position has a strong tendency to become a palatalized [ʎ] in Catalan:

| Latin LUNAM (moon) | French *lune* | Catalan *lluna* | Spanish *luna* |

In medial position, laterals are more stable, although sometimes they become weak or even palatalized:

| Latin FILIOLUM (son) | Portuguese *filhó* | Catalan *fill* | Spanish *hijo* |

In other contexts, there is a metathesis of the vibrant:

| Latin QUATTUOR (four) | Catalan *quatre* | Spanish *cuatro* |

We also find assimilation or dissimilation with <l-r>.

BARCINONE   Barcelona

Regarding nasals, in Iberian texts we find a representation of two or three different graphemes. The labial <m> is the least present, while the dental nasal <n> is more abundant and stable. Interestingly enough, pronunciation in the proto-Romances also shows this tendency to convert the nasal labial to dental. In Catalan, in final position it disappears.

| Latin REM (nothing) | French *rien* | Catalan *re* | Spanish *nada* |

| Latin QUEM (who) | French *qui* | Catalan *qui* | Spanish *quien* |

The nasal consonant <n> has the characteristic of modifying its manner of articulation according to the consonant preceding or following it. The case of the palatal nasal [ɲ], already introduced when we discussed the alphabet, is perhaps one of the most curious. We should remember that Latin did not have a palatal nasal consonant, whereas it is found in all Romance languages. Transcribed with different graphemes, the same pronunciation is used for Spanish *español*, Catalan *espanyol*, French *espagnol*, Italian *spagnolo* and Portuguese *espanhol*.

The palatal nasal is found in three articulatory contexts:

- Under the action of a yod (palatal vowel) on the preceding nasal, the manner of articulation of the consonant is modified towards the palate:

| Latin SENIOREM (sir) | Spanish *señor* | Catalan *senyor* |

- A velar consonant <k, g> followed by a nasal consonant <n> is articulated in a fricative way and moves the manner of articulation towards the palate. In Catalan, the tendency is so strong that both consonants, the initial lateral <l> and the <gn> group, are palatalized:

| Latin LIGNA (firewood) | Spanish *leña* | Catalan *llenya* |

- By contact of a double or geminate nasal consonant <mn, nn>:

| Latin AUTUMNUM (autumn) | Spanish *otoño* |

Since these articulations are explained time and again by palatalization, a very common and important phenomenon in the Romances, please refer to the explanations given in previous chapters.

4.12 Consonant groups

Geminate or double consonants in medial position, such as <cc, dd, ll, mm, nn, rr, ss, tt>, are a very common Latin feature, as already mentioned. They tend to be simplified, except in the cases discussed above. In the orthography, some literary words have preserved this spelling.

When the consonants are different, the following occurs:

- Occlusive + liquid: there are several possible combinations, the consonant clusters have been voiced or reduced according to the different articulatory contexts. For example:

    - Unvoiced stops, clusters <pl, pr, tr, cr>, tend to be voiced:

Latin DUPLUM (double)	Spanish and Catalan *doble*	French *double*
Latin CAPRA (goat)	Spanish and Catalan *cabra*	French *chèvre*
Latin PETRA (stone)	Spanish *piedra*	Catalan *pedra*
Latin LACRIMA (tear)	Spanish *lágrima*	Catalan *llàgrima*

- Voiced stops, groups <dr, gr>, lose the occlusive:

Latin QUADRAGINTA (forty)	Spanish *cuarenta*	Catalan *quaranta*
Latin PIGRITIA (laziness)	Spanish *pereza*	Catalan *peresa*

- Two stops, clusters <ct, pt>, are modified by assimilation and palatalization:

Latin OCTO (eight)	Italian *otto*	Spanish *ocho*	Catalan *vuit*
Latin SEPTEM (seven)	Italian *sette*	Spanish *siete*	Catalan *set*

• In Latin, vibrant + sibilant, cluster <rs>, was assimilated to <r> but the Romances prefer <s>:

Latin URSU (bear)	Spanish *oso*	Catalan *ós*

Muta cum liquida (occlusive plus liquid) consonant clusters were very abundant in Latin; nevertheless, they are not found in Iberian or in Basque. We believe this is important: it is perhaps one of the characteristics that allow us to establish the separation of the proto-Romance languages from the Indo-European trunk at a date prior to Latin – which brings them closer, due to their affinity, to old Mediterranean languages such as Cretan and other ancient Hellenic languages.

4.13 Suppression of sounds

In medieval texts we find vowel elisions when the final vowel of a word is in contact with the initial vowel of the following word. In Catalan, this phenomenon is very frequent and is regulated by modern spelling rules through apostrophes or hyphens. In the study of Iberian, possible elisions and orthographic variations are not usually taken into account but we assume they were quite common. Moreover, in many epigraphies the text is written in continuous segments, without separation blanks between words, so it would be more appropriate to consider that Iberian writing represents phonotactic units and not syllables and isolated words.

Apheresis	Syncope	Apocope
—	—	—

- Apheresis means loss of an initial phoneme or syllable.

  This feature is very common in the proto-Romances.

  In Catalan names, there is an enormous amount of 'Catalan-style' hypocoristic shortened nicknames:

  > Joaquim > Quim; Francesc > Cesc
  > Eulàlia > Laia; Josefina > Fina

- Syncope means loss of a vowel sound inside a word, which can reduce the number of syllables.

  This loss is found in consonant groups simplified by suppression of the weaker element, usually the one in medial position. In Spanish, the syllable was redistributed and closed codas could become open. In Catalan, closed codas have been better preserved and the tendency is to have a final apocope.

- Apocope means suppression of the unstressed final part of a word.

  One of the prominent features of Catalan is the generalized apocope of unstressed post-tonic syllables, showing a clear preference for closed syllable codas. In Spanish, the tendency for an open syllable preserves the final syllable, while preventing the apocope:

| Latin AMICUM (friend) | Spanish *amigo* | Catalan *amic* |

Other instances of suppression of sounds are:

- Elision, where, by contact between the final or the initial vowel of a word, one of the vowels is elided.
- Crasis, i.e. the fusion of two vowels, one final and one initial, when two words merge into one.

Both are typical phenomena of spoken language and are very present in some Romances. We also find them in Greek.

4.14 Addition of sounds

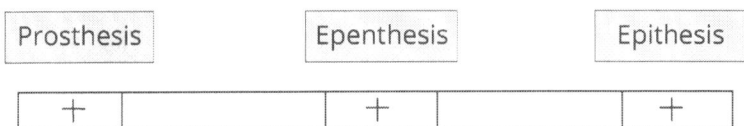

- Prosthesis means addition of a vowel element at the beginning of a word.

This phenomenon is detected in written language in the 2nd Century AD; with the prosthetic vowel <i-> that, from the 2nd to the 7th Century, evolved to <e-> until becoming an integral part of the word.

| Latin /Greek SCHOLAM (school) | Spanish *escuela* | Catalan *escola* |

The first example of a prosthetic vowel is an inscription from the 2nd Century AD, found in Barcelona, which mentions *ispumosus* instead of *spumosus*. Other prosthetic vowel testimonies are found in Greek words beginning with a sibilant or consonant cluster <sm, sp, sc>:

| Greek SMARAGDUS (emerald) | ismaragdus |

Greek SPIRITUS (spirit)   espíritu

- Epenthesis means insertion inside a word of a non-etymological consonant or vowel phoneme. Anaptixis is a type of epenthesis that consists of the addition of a vowel to facilitate its pronunciation, and usually corresponds to a literary word or a hypercorrection.

Pre-Romance:

Carbassa (pumpkin) > Spanish *calabaza*; Catalan *carabassa* or *carbassa*

This addition turns the closed coda into an open one.

CHAPTER 5

5.1 Lexicology

Historical linguistics is based on the comparative method for studying the diachronic evolution of languages and their possible genetic relationship. Comparative grammar looks for similarities between words of different languages in order to establish their kinship, origin and evolution. In addition to establishing regular phonetic correspondences, morphosyntactic features are studied and a search is made for cognates, i.e. similar words that can refer to a common origin. Thus, words are grouped according to their semantic fields and compared. Formal resemblance may be a coincidence, a loan between languages in contact or a transmission by inheritance. In the case of Romance languages, the number of words that belong exclusively to each of the Romance languages is very limited. In fact, Romance languages share much of their vocabulary with Latin, which is why the similarity has been attributed to a relation of filiation. At no time has the possibility of a kinship that does not stem from Latin been considered. The similarities to English and German again lead us back to a common language, hypothetically reconstructed, that has been called Indo-European. Beyond Indo-European, the search for a common origin is still alive, because we often find that, for example, in Hebrew (a Semitic language from the Afro-Asiatic family), consonants coincide.

I contend that the etymological generalization and affinity of the lexicon of Romance languages goes far beyond Latin and links back to another parent tongue, a *koiné* of higher chronology. Words are the sound representation of symbolic elements: they point to how its speakers thought, felt and lived. When different peoples share similar cultural and social elements, when their ideas are the same, the result is formally related words (lexemes). But let us not get ahead of ourselves. I will elaborate on these concepts in the following chapters.

First of all, I would like to draw attention not so much to the apparent similarity between languages but to the differences, especially when they occur within the very basic vocabulary. We will see that the vocabulary of Romance languages is different from that of Latin.

Following are some words that:

- belong to the same semantic field; and
- have not been affected by phonetic transformations.

I have chosen the semantic field of war because Romans were conquerors and what they did most and best was fighting. Therefore, it is surprising that not only has there not been lexical a transfer from Latin to Romance languages within this field but Romance languages have managed to preserve, amongst themselves, a common vocabulary foreign to Latin:

Catalan	Spanish	French	Italian	Romanian	Latin
Tractat	Tratado	Traité	Trattato	Tratat	FOEDUS
Ostatge	Rehén	Otage	Ostaggio	Ostatic	OBSES
Guerra	Guerra	Guerre	Guerra	Război	BELLUM
Desastre	Desastre	Désastre	Disastro	Dezastru	CLADES
Lluita	Lucha	Lutte	Lotta	Luptă	PUGNA
Flota	Flota	Flotte	Flotta	Flotă	CLASSIS
Bronze	Bronce	Bronze	Bronzo	Bronz	AES
Esclau	Esclavo	Esclave	Schiavo	Sclav	SERVUS
General	General	Général	Generale	General	IMPERATOR
Brau	Bravo	Brave	Bravo	Brav	PROBUS
Casc	Casco	Casque	Casco	Cască	GALEA
Orfe	Huérfano	Orphelin	Orfano	Orfan	ORBUS
Cop	Golpe	Coup	Colpo	Lovitură	ICTUS
Galop	Galope	Galop	Galoppo	Galop	CURSUS
Matança	Matanza	Massacre	Massacro	Masacru	CAEDES
Maça	Maza	Massue	Mazza	Măciucă	CLAVA

We have reproduced the table on p. 41-42 of the book by Yves Cortez,[75] so we have respected his translations.[76]

---

75 CORTEZ, YVES. *Le français ne vient pas du latin!* L'Harmattan Publisher (2007), p. 41.

76 It is interesting to take into account the form documented in ancient Romanian (information provided by Mihaela Alda):

war – răzbel/rezbel (modern Romanian: *război*).

general – ghinărar/ghenerar (modern Romanian: *general*)

massacre – măcel/mesernița/mesarniță (modern Romanian *masacru*)

mace – mai (modern Romanian: *măciucă*)

As we can see in this table, there are very few words in each language that are different from the rest. But, it is also clear that we can use other synonyms to force a similarity. For example, we can say that the word GENERAL exists in Latin, although its meaning has nothing to do with an army general, since in Latin the terms DUX or IMPERATOR were used preferentially. This lexical-semantic change is usually explained by analogy or metonymy. Strangely, in all Romance languages this change occurred in exactly the same way, which shows that their way of thinking and their psychological classifications coincided, while at the same time being different from the Latin mentality.

Moreover, we constantly find inconsistencies. If we look up the word *espada* (sword) in a Spanish etymological dictionary, it traces the origin to the Latin SPATHA, which in turn comes from the Greek SPATHE. However, the Romans (those who could speak Latin) used the words GLADIUS (short double edged sword), ENSIS (weapon of war), PUGIO (military dagger) or SICA (dagger).

A paradigm of inconsistency is the word *slave*.[77] Etymological dictionaries mention that it comes from the Latin SCLAVUS. The Larousse dictionary gives the following etymology: «vient du latin médiéval SCLAVUS de SLAVUS (Slave)» and explains that the Germans reduced many Slavs to slavery. The etymological evolution is explained through a very complicated evolution that involves the mysterious appearance of a non-etymological, epenthetic sound [k] that can be found in all languages, because slave in German is *Sklave*, in Catalan *esclau*, in French *esclave*, in Italian *schiavo*, in Romanian *sclav*.[78] How is it possible for something to be so incredibly exceptional? All languages added the same non-etymological [k] sound! And, supposedly, they all did it in the Middle Ages, when sadly slavery is much older! Obviously, the Romans were not expected to capture Slavs to designate it! The pity is that in Latin a slave was called SERVUS, so this explanation verges on the ridiculous.

The Larousse dictionary, like so many others, picks up a popular etymology that is the result of a paronym, i.e. an error produced or induced by a mere similarity of hearing.

---

77 CORTEZ, YVES. *Le français ne vient pas du latin!* L'Harmattan Publisher (2007), p. 89.

78 In Romanian, *slave* is 'sclav', and *Slav*, 'slav', but there is also the word 'slab' (with its dialect variant 'sclab', with the epenthesis of <c>), meaning 'weak' or 'thin'. Despite the formal similarity, it must be taken into account that in Romanian phonemes [b] and [v] are not confused: the first is a bilabial stop and the second is a voiced fricative.

Yves Cortez gives a different explanation: it is a word composed by ESC-LAVE where EX is a prefix[79] (the same as in *ex-husband*) and LAVE is a lexeme related to LABOR, synonymous with work but which includes a semantic nuance of decent work. The slave was the person excluded from decent work and forced to perform the most ungrateful work.

Classical Latin	False etymology	Etymology
liquid + consonant + vowel **LCV**	VL#C[k]LV#CV	Prefix **EX** + **LABOR**
SLAVO (S + LA + VO)	ES + [k] LA + VO [es 'kla βo]	EX + LABOR [la'βor] ≠ ['la βo]

We wish to add two observations that make us appreciate the etymology of Yves Cortez as another avenue to be explored:

If we take into account the explanation about the stress, Latin had no oxytone words. Thus, by Latinizing it, the word [la'βor] becomes a paroxytone ['la βo].

The change in the Latin stress should have brought about a change in the syllable structure. However, it did not, and all languages maintain the main stress on the first syllable, which proves that it is a prefix (EX).

However, in Romance languages the phonemes [b] and [v] are not confused. In Catalan, in the word *esclau*, [v] has become [u], while the word *labor* keeps the [b], which shows that the sounds [b] and [v] are not always homophones.

The true etymology of the word *esclavo* cannot be related to the Slavs, but to its formants: ESK-KA-LA-VO.

The hypothesis of philologist Núria Garcia Quera[80] is quite in line with Yves Cortez. However, she analyses separately not only the lexeme EX but all the formants of the word, which leads us to an even more suggestive conclusion.

Formant ES (which can be found as EX- or ES-) is common in different languages, with exactly the same meaning. Thus, in Spanish it means 'outside' or 'beyond', in relation to space or time. Examples: *extender, extraer,*

---

79 Prefix meaning deprivation in the sense of 'outside', 'beyond', "that was and has ceased to be" (Dictionary of the Spanish Language, DRAE).

80 Núria Garcia Quera is a philologist specialized in toponymy and a writer very well acquainted with the landscape of the Pyrenees. She has published many mountain guides. We have studied together and are both researching and developing this new hypothesis. For more information, see http://www.sensus.cat/

exhumar, excéntrico. It also means "that was and has ceased to be". Examples: *expresidente, exmarido*. In Catalan: "Prefix indicating that someone has stopped being what the root says. Examples: *exdiputat, exministre*. Prefix which means 'on the outside'. Ex.: *exosquelet, exodermis, excèntric*." In French: "il marque la sortie, la séparation, le point de départ, ce qu'un être vivant, une chose concrète ou abstraite, etc. ont été et ce qu'elles ont cessé d'être". And in English: "out of, away from, lacking, former". Examples: *exit, exhale, exclusive, exceed, explosion, ex-mayor...* Therefore, EX gives us an idea of something 'alien', of something "that was and has ceased to be" in relation to the rest of the word, which matches the hypothesis of Yves Cortez.

The second formant, phoneme [k], as we have studied, corresponds to 'rock' and, at the same time, to a 'living creature'. Note that in Spanish it is common in many animal names, and we also find it in the parts of the human body:

- Semantic field of fauna: **ca**bra, **ca**ballo, **ga**to, **ca**racol, es**ca**rabajo, **ca**mello, va**ca**, **ca**imán, **ca**chalote, **ca**lamar, **ca**ngrejo... (*goat, horse, cat, snail, beetle, camel, cow, alligator, sperm whale, squid, crab...*)
- Semantic field of the human body: bo**ca**, **ca**beza, **ca**bello, **ca**deras, **ca**ra, muñe**ca**, nu**ca**... (*mouth, head, hair, hips, face, wrist, nape...*)

Therefore, the fact that the word *esclavo* (slave) carries the phoneme [k], and that it can be found in different languages, is an indication that the word refers to a 'human being'.

Formant LA (that can be found as L, LA, LL, LLA; in other languages, the consonant phoneme [l] or [ʎ] may be accompanied by other vowels) always refers to 'related to', 'united', 'tied', 'bound', 'subject', 'linked', and so on.

Therefore, we know so far that the word ES C LA is referring to "something that was and has stopped being", to 'human' and to 'linked'. There is still the last part, formant -VO, -U, -V or -VE, depending on the language. This is the consonantal or semi-consonantal phoneme that displays the most variety in this word, although always as fricatives or labial approximants. When this sound is found at the end of a word, it usually has the meaning of 'formerly' (see, for example, the past tense of verbs), but when we find it after LA, LLA it acquires the meaning of 'negation', so it would be 'unbound' or 'free'.

As a result, and bearing in mind that we are talking about an agglutinative language that must be interpreted from right to left, and that the first part of the word (EX) acts as a modifier of the rest of the word, the meaning of ESCLAVO (slave) would be:

ESCLAVO> ES C LA VO = 'formerly' + 'free human'

The lexicon is the most widely studied part of comparative linguistics. It is also the most volatile part of a language, since every historical period corresponds to a massive lexical movement of certain semantic fields. And yet lexical changes are not always logical. For example, in Spanish, why do we say *caballo* (horse) and not EQVVS, and yet for the female we have maintained *yegua* (mare), in Catalan *euga*, in Romanian *iapă*, in Sardinian *èbba*, and in Portuguese *égua*? In addition, some of the words the Romance languages had dropped were borrowed again from Classical Latin much later, so we combine words from different origins and at different stages of evolution. Following the previous example, why is horse riding called *equitación* (equestrianism) in Spanish?

In historical grammar, migrationism theory is accepted as an axiom: the population spread in one direction, from east to west, through successive migratory waves.[81] As the populations moved away from the original nucleus, languages became more diversified, moving away from the primordial language. Thus, the different language families emerged. Comparative grammar attempts to recompose these linguistic families by reconstructing the process in reverse, going from the branches to the common trunk. Thus, the so-called Romance languages would share a common parent language that has been identified with Latin and, following the same theoretical design, a regression has been made to the Copper Age cultures, where a language called Indo-European (IE) would hypothetically have been spoken.

Who were the Indo-Europeans? Georges Dumézil[82] established the explanatory model of Indo-European societies based on three social strata: authority, war, and productivity. This model enjoys great recognition today; it is generally accepted that the Indo-Europeans were the first sedentary societies with an advanced civilization. Going back to the second millennium BC, they built large cities - supported by agriculture and organized by the ruling classes, with kings and priests (interpreters of the divinity), armies, free workers and slaves.

---

81 Archaeologist Colin Renfrew defends the hypothesis that the Indo-European languages spread due to the expansion of agriculture from Anatolia. Others, such as linguist Francisco Villar, support the Kurgan theory proposed by Marija Gimbutas, which establishes the origin of Indo-European in the Balkans.

82 Georges Dumézil, (1898-1986), French philologist and historian, made a contribution that has been considered crucial in the study of Indo-European societies and religions. He established a structure based on a society divided into three social strata: the sacred-juridical function, the war function, and the production function.

Such a society is associated with two concepts: sedentarism; and war for resources, which theoretically entails mass invasions and massive migrations set in motion because of famines, cataclysms, or pure expansionism (the right of conquest). This involved fierce confrontations resulting in thousands of people being killed; later increased by looting, rape and pillage and a by hard life for the survivors, who would have to endure cruel atrocities. We have seen this in movies. And yet, was this what really happened? So much has been written about Indo-European that it is often forgotten it is only a theoretical framework. In *The Art of War*, published in 513 BC, the author Sun Tzu, a Chinese military strategist, gives some clues showing how it is impossible for such a system of military invasions and massive migrations to expand for centuries. Long wars have never benefited the expansion of peoples. Had they existed, Indo-Europeans would have been doomed to failure unless they had legitimate political and moral authority. And, for that, you need more than just strategy. Plenty of food and excellent logistics are required. Sun Tzu said:

> «Raising a host of a hundred thousand men and marching them great distances entails heavy loss on the people and a drain on the resources of the State. The daily expenditure will amount to a thousand ounces of silver. There will be commotion at home and abroad, and men will drop down exhausted on the highways. As many as seven hundred thousand families will be impeded in their labour.»

If the dynamics of group logistics are studied with sufficient information and criteria, boundaries arise immediately, showing how it might be possible for a cavalry corps to advance rapidly and to survive providing it went through rich farmlands and the colonists continued to work (willingly or unwillingly) for the invader. But such an advance would not have been possible for groups of more than a couple of hundred people when crossing steppes, forests or other taigas that had low specific productivity.

Therefore, would such an advance have been possible if the locals chose to burn the land and scatter across a large area to survive precariously, taking to the hills? It is impossible to claim that there were large migrations, unless they were divided into smaller groups and were consistent with the production rhythms of nature or the seasonal migrations of large ungulates. Transhumance has been practised extensively and for thousands of years in certain geographical areas whose biomes were based on meadows, pastures and forests not as dense as the rain forests.[83]

Our research leads us to suggest a different hypothesis. We believe that there was no 'original nucleus'. As before agriculture people had to move, they followed the seasons and crossed entire continents. So, from the Paleolithic, migrations were manifold in all directions. This dynamic was like a large sieve that, favoured by a migratory lifestyle, continuously blended cultural contributions and favoured genetic interbreeding. Technologies, beliefs, lifestyles and (particularly) a shared language were assets that created homogeneous languages: the same symbolic language, a similar way of understanding life, of thinking and feeling. This asset began to decline precisely with the rise of local agriculture/husbandry and sedentary lifestyle. In just a few millennia, borders were a fact – and, with them, the mobility disappeared, thus causing the lost of the uniformity factor of the languages. So it was really sedentarism that led to the isolation of different populations and their speeches: hence, diversification.

When an isolated language suddenly blends with others, lexical transfers occur, the syntax is altered, the keys of its symbolism are lost and the language starts to be governed by laws of phonetic analogy, weakening the relationship with the second level of language, which is symbolic. We then fall into the trap of identifying lexemes as the only significant part of words, and of defining affixes or compositional elements as mere grammatical components. However, this conception relates to a theoretical descriptive model which creates much confusion.

Let us now discuss etymology.

5.2 Etymology

Etymology is a part of historical linguistics that studies the origin of words. We could think of it as the archaeology of language, as it shows us the evolution and structural changes that could bring us closer to this supposed ancient language. Etymology can also help us to detect the mental processes as reflected in the evolution of language. If we study them, we can see that these

---

[83] Information extracted from the article by Javier Goitia: *El pastel indoeuropeo se hornea sin la guinda del Euskera* (The Indo-European cake is baked without the icing of the Euskera language), presented at a monographic conference on the Indo-European organized by Euskararen Jatorria and celebrated in Zestoa on May 9, 2015. It can be consulted online at:

http://euskararenjatorria.net/wp-content/uploads/2015/06/Euskeraren_Jatorria_10_Biltzarra_05_Jabier_Goitia_Blanco.pdf changes are not as random or whimsical as Saussure[84] suggested, but rather regular; they are applied with perfect mathematical accuracy, so it becomes evident that they follow internal norms. Trouble is, we do not always know how to explain these norms. Interestingly, historical grammar constrains etymologies so that they can fit into its theoretical idea of evolution.

In languages that have a long written tradition, etymology studies texts to find the evolutionary stages of words. Since Latin was the only language written in Europe throughout the Middle Ages, it is assumed that Latin was the parent tongue of all current Romance languages. This prevents researchers from considering a possible origin that does not include Latin. Consequently, etymological dictionaries refer to Latin to explain the origin of most words. The names of towns and cities, toponyms, anthroponyms, but also all the common vocabulary introduced in official texts, were either adapted to the Latin language or replaced by neologisms created from Latin. With these often grotesque changes, words were separated from their true etymology and meaning.

Another issue that adds complexity to this research is orthography. Historical grammar speaks of *dead letters* (elisions) that are lost or transformed throughout the existence of a word, thus justifying the linguistic change and the evolution of languages. The institutions that protect and establish the orthographic principles of languages[85] have decided that silent letters should be preserved because they refer to their linguistic heritage, to their etymology. This has led to the existence of languages whose spelling is very different from their pronunciation, such as French and English. But it has also achieved the opposite effect to the intended, because current writing inevitably leads us away from the true origin of words. Spelling seems to deliberately seek justification for Latin or for the alleged Indo-European etymology, distorting the true meaning and obscuring explanations based on a parent language of pre-Roman origin.

Prescriptive grammar dictates the rules of orthography. Observing the rules does not mean that these are correct or unquestionable. Text messages on cell phones are an overwhelming example of the use of language. Accents and <h> are deleted, consonants are used as they sound (<ll> becomes

---

84 Swiss linguist Ferdinand de Saussure (1857-1913) is considered the father of modern linguistics. His book *Course in General Linguistics* (1916), published posthumously by his students, laid the foundations of structuralism.

85 In Spain, the *Royal Academy of the Spanish Language (RAE)*, or its equivalent institution in different countries

<y>, <q, c> become <k>), advantage is taken of vowel sounds associated with consonants, and vowels are eliminated (kdmos? = quedamos? – 'shall we meet?'); also, signs and emoticons that reduce the number of words are introduced. Young people are changing the relationship between signifier and meaning by applying a new arbitrary relationship (according to Saussure's principles!), and thus they are creating a new code, with new rules that allow them to write quickly, using only two fingers. This has emerged spontaneously by applying the Principle of Linguistic Economy, which is one of the universal laws of linguistics! It is fair to assume that all writings have emerged in this same way: the sender uses a series of signs to encode a message and send it to the receiver. As soon as a technological innovation that enhances and facilitates this communication appears, it is only logical that it should replace and displace the earlier writing methods.[86]

Let us have a look at some examples of these false etymologies and how orthography can distort the origin and the semantic relationship of words belonging to the same lexical family.

We are told that the word *invocar* (invoke) comes from the Latin etymon INVOCARE and means 'asking for help or assistance'. This help is undoubtedly requested using one's mouth, by naming or calling someone with one's voice. The etymological origin should then relate **boca** (mouth) with **boca**do (bite), **voz** (voice) and **voca**blo (word). However, orthography distinguishes between words written with <b> or with <v>, thus obscuring the possibility of a common etymon. Let us consider one more example. The word **respons**abilidad (responsibility) derives from the verb **respon**der (to respond). Responsibility is the ability to give and assume an answer. **Hábil** (skilful; is a word related to the English word 'able' – 'to be able to'), which is in turn related to **hab**er (to have). We call *hábil* the person who can easily *tener* (have) or **ob**tener (obtain), and so who has **apt**itud (aptitude), because he is **apt**o (able). Therefore, the etymological relationship between *responsabilidad (*respond and ability*)*, and between *aptitud* and *obtener (*aptitude and obtain*)* should be visible in their spelling.

What is there behind words?

Our analysis of words cannot be limited to the first linguistic level, of phonetic similarity. If we really look deeper into the etymology (into the meaning of words), we will immediately realize that there is a second level, related to the first.. This second level shows a pictorial value or symbolic significance,

---

86 Filología de la A a la Z (A to Z Philology), https://www.youtube.com/watch?v=5acn6J_5oCo&app=desktop

which represents one of the new lines of research in cognitive grammar, developed by American linguist Ronald Langacker[87].

> Cognitive linguistics assumes a symbolic basis for all grammatical constructs. Constructs are conglomerates of information put together to form a unit that speakers use to understand and produce a language. This allows us to go beyond regarding language as simple structures (like Lego pieces) that combine at grammatical level, and instead consider symbols as the basic unit, combining a semantic structure with a phonological label.

Bearing these new concepts in mind, what languages share and what is transmitted from one to another would not so much be the phonetic evolution of a word but the idea, the meaning it conveys. Languages share a symbolism; therefore, what is important is not to determine if the lexemes of a language have stemmed and evolved phonetically from words of another language but to understand that they come from the same initial concept, the same meaning or symbol.

Here are some eloquent examples:

The word *perdón* (forgiveness) is made up of 'para' + 'dar ' (in Latin, PERDONARE = 'per' + 'donare'). It is made up the same way in Spanish as it is in English, despite using different elements: *forgive* is the sum of 'for' + 'give'. If we look for the word *perdonar* in an etymological dictionary, we are referred back to Latin and the general meaning is of "someone resigning voluntarily from punishing a fault, crime or offense". And yet the literal meaning of the components has a much more profound sense than that of a *voluntary resignation*. The amazing thing is finding in two languages from different families the same idea that *to forgive you must give*. This happens more often than we might think.

The word *night*, in many languages, is formed by 'n' + 'eight':

---

[87] American linguist Ronald Langacker is known especially for his role in the development of cognitive linguistics. He argues that all grammatical constructs can be formed by three types of units: semantic, phonological and symbolic. The symbolic being those that associate semantic and phonological units at the same time.

Spanish	noche =	n + ocho
Catalan	nit =	n + vuit
French	nuit =	n + huit
Portuguese, Galician	noite =	n + oito
Italian	notte =	n + otto
Romanian	noapte =	n + opt
English	night =	n + eight
German	nacht =	n + acht
Norwegian	natt =	n + atte
Latin	nox, noctis =	n + octo
Greek	νύχτα =	ν + οκτώ

What does this mean? What explanation can we give? Is it a coincidence? What connotations and symbolism associated with the number eight connect it with the night? Night is when there is no light, when we do not see. It literally means not seeing (*no ojo* = no eye). But why is *ocho* (eight) related with *noche* (night), and *nueve* (nine) with *nuevo* (new)?

How is it possible?

At a subconscious level, languages establish subtle ties that act in the formation of words by creating relationships in the figurative sense. Rhetoric defines them as tropes (deviation from the original meaning), which are widely used in literary language. Here are some tropes:

- A *synecdoche* uses the whole for a part of something or a part for the whole: e.g. 'a thousand souls' instead of 'a thousand people'; 'the steel' for 'the sword'.

- A *metaphor* acts by similarity and analogy, changing the direct (literal) meaning for a figurative one.

- A *metonymy* designates something using the name of something else, substituting (for instance) the effect for the cause, the sign for the thing it means, the author for the work.

This ability of language explains that, over time, there are words that have transmuted their meaning. We all agree on this. However, dictionaries seem to ignore these processes because it is considered that they move us away from the true origin and meaning of words.

Let us have a look at what kind of information contained in words may go beyond the apparent and official significance given in a dictionary. I will soon explain the reason for doing this.

The Spanish word *abandonar* (to abandon), according to the dictionary of Maria Moliner,[88] comes from the French 'abandonner' and means "to leave aside something that one has the obligation to take care of or to attend to, moving or not away from it". Since it is evident that it is part of the same family as **banc**o (bank, bench), **banc***al* (terrace), **band***a* (band), **band***eja* (tray), **band***era* (flag, banner) or **band***o* (group, bunch), we look for these words in the same etymological dictionary. *Banco* comes from the Germanic 'bank' and means seat. *Bancal* comes from the Arabic 'manqála' and means support. *Banda* comes from the Germanic 'Band' and means a tape, ribbon or strip made from flexible material. *Bandeja* comes from Portuguese and means a flat serving tray. *Bando* comes from the Gothic 'bandwo' which means a flag, and also a gathering of people or "group of people fighting against others or against opposing ideas". With this contradictory information that refers us to different languages (Arabic, Germanic, Gothic, French, Portuguese), it is impossible to see that all these words are based on a common idea (or concept) of group or union. Thus, by analogy with **band***a* (*band,* a group of yarns that forms a flexible tape), the concept of **band***o* (*band* of people) is created, as well as that of a *musical band*, and their **band***era* (flag) is the cloth that represents them, while a set of assembled planks on which (unlike a chair) several people can sit, is a **banc***o* (bench). Let us return now to the word *abandonar* and address its original meaning: to leave out of a group or 'band'. To understand this we do not need to know French, Arabic or Gothic. Just a little common sense...

> What we find is that there is a meaning – a metaphysical or philosophical idea – hidden in words.

As if there was a metalanguage, we find a hidden meaning within the formal meaning, like a sublanguage within the language, which would provide us with new information (at a second level), and which our subconscious recognizes and knows how to interpret. We are talking about a symbolic encrypted language that refers us directly to the idea, the concept, and uses a code we have forgotten at a conscious level. Everything seems to indicate that this meaning has been universal.

---

88 MOLINER, MARÍA. *Diccionario del uso del español*, I-II. Editorial Gredos, S.A. Madrid (1999).

Let us look at another example that illustrates this deep, almost magical level of meaning. The words *afecto* (affection) (María Moliner: from Latin AFFECTUS, -A, -UM) and *efecto* (effect) (Maria Moliner: from the Latin EFFECTUS, numeral and partitive) share the same idea of *hecho* (in Spanish; **fet**s in Catalan; 'fact' in English). The difference is that some *facts* are internal and emotional and start with <a> because they *affect me*, while others are external and physical and start with <e> because they are *outside me*. Unravelling this thread a little more, *defecto* (defect) is a no-effect or negative effect; *efectivo* (effective) is what produces an effect and *eficaz* (efficient) is that which produces much effect or the desired effect; *eferente* (efferent) applies to some outwardly oriented thing; and *infección* (infection) is an infected effect. On the other hand, *afectos* (affections) that *affect* us and provoke feelings or attitudes cause us *afecciones* (affections) that are also infected affects, because the term is used when the health of an organ is altered and we become ill. I am saying all this to you *afectuosamente* (affectionately), which literally means with an affectionate affable mind, teeming with feeling.

Another example: We are told that the Spanish word *amigo* (friend) comes from the Latin AMICUS. However, if we pay attention to the formants, we can see it is composed of three monosyllables 'a' + 'mi' + 'co' which literally means 'the one who is with me'. Isn't that a friend, the one who is next to me, the one who shows me his *affection*?

And another: *Anillo* (ring) (María Moliner: from the Latin ANELLUS, diminutive of ANULUS) and *año* (year) (María Moliner: from the Latin ANNUS) contain the same symbolic idea, because a year closes a cycle or ring, a complete revolution around the sun. And what is a ring but a closed object in the form of a circle? Language symbolically refers to a **an**illo de boda (wedding ring) or to the **an**ular (annular; finger where the ring is placed); to something **an**ejo (inherent, relative; united in a close relationship), or **an**exo (annexed; attached to something). And won't the affix '–ano' (that in Spanish makes up derived adjectives turning into a quality the meaning of the noun from which it derives), have the same origin? Thus, *ciudadano* (citizen) is someone who belongs to the circle of the *ciudad* (city), *Sevillano* (Sevillian) belongs to the circle of *Sevilla*, *serrano* (mountain-dweller) to the *sierra* (mountain), *hortelano* (gardener) to the *huerto* (orchard), *cirujano* (surgeon) to *cirugía* (surgery)… This seems logical, doesn't it? Well, so it should. But if we look up the word *ciudadano* (citizen) in an ethimological dictionary, it sends us to the Latin CIVILIS, -E, and *ciudad* (city) refers to CIVITAS, -ATIS, disregarding what seems to be obvious. And we could continue with all the words in the dictionary, a work that we have been doing for some years now, becoming more and more amazed at how precise and astonishing a language can be.

For many years I have wondered how this metalanguage works. The answer goes in the following direction: the brain makes no distinction between what it sees and what it imagines. The earliest words (lexemes) tended to describe what was seen. A word was equal to an idea; consider some of the first referents, e.g. body parts. In Catalan, the word **cost**a (coast) has the same beginning as the word **cos** (body); **cost**ella (rib) and **cost**at (side) are parts of this **cos**. Joining two pieces or bodies of something is **cos**ir (to sew). To bring something towards us is *acostar* (to bring closer). In Spanish, *brazos* (arms) are used to *abrazar* (to embrace). *Manos* (hands) are used to *amasar* (to knead). *Pies* (feet) are used to *pedalear* (to pedal). Falling on one's *rodillas* (knees) is *arrodillarse* (to kneel). A *dedal* (thimble) is worn on the *dedo* (finger). And the *collar* (necklace), on the *cuello* (neck). A large *bota* (wineskin) is called *barril* (barrel) because it is like a large *barriga* (belly). We use our *cabeza* (head) for a *cabezazo* (header; masculine noun, voluntary movement) or for a *cabezada* (nap; feminine noun, involuntary movement), and someone stubborn is called *cabezón* (headstrong).

When language goes one step further to describe what cannot be seen, it applies exactly the same method, relating concepts with visual metaphors. It uses imagination.

If we look at the word *imagination*, it is related to 'image'. Imagination, an abstract concept, is the ability to create mental images. Surprisingly, the literal interpretation of its formants is the sum of 'image' + 'action'; imagination is the first step for the creation of our reality, because it sets in motion the energy necessary to put into practice and fix a vibration so that it takes shape and materializes. Imagination means *images in action*. This is what quantum physics is demonstrating. This word is much older than quantum physics; and yet the depth, precision and wisdom of the sum of its formants and its meaning are unquestionable. Incredible, isn't it?

Imagination is activated by metaphorical language, creating relationships between the visible and the non-visible world. For example, the visible activity of eating and the whole process of food assimilation allow us to describe perceptible but invisible psychological states. Thus, metaphorically: when we do not like a person, we cannot *stomach* him or her, just as we do not *stomach* a lie; when we need to think a lot about something, we *ruminate* on it, as if we needed to chew it well; *ruminating*, metaphorically, also means grumbling; we have difficulty *digesting* a dislike or the death of a loved one; when something definitely does not feel good, it is *indigestible* or ends up causing us a *bellyache* and, if things become even more serious, we do not *give a shit*, literally letting go of all our discomfort. According to traditional grammar, metaphors are a way of taking advantage of figurative words, an aesthetic way of using the language that is usually considered a stylistic and literary resource. Cognitive grammar has completely changed this perception. Lakoff[89] and Johnson[90] established that metaphors are part of the cognitive processes, i.e. humans think by associating concepts in a metaphorical language, and therefore a metaphor is a tool of knowledge inherent to learning.

Who created words? Did they really arise by chance? And were they assigned indiscriminately, based on conventions? How are we supposed to have moved from the onomatopoeic grunt to the metaphor? And more importantly: is this linguistic capacity being used properly, or is it being intentionally manipulated? Teun van Dijk[91] states that the latter is indeed so; language is used as a tool for social manipulation.[92]

Beyond this new etymology conception that we have set forth, do we actually have any proof of the existence of this ancient language, of agglutinative nature, that combined (monosyllabic) lexical units corresponding to concepts and ideas? Of course we do! We are surrounded by evidence! Many of the formants of this language have survived in today's languages. Where we will see them best is in the toponymy.

---

[89] George Lakoff is an American linguist and professor at the University of California, Berkeley. A researcher of cognitive linguistics, he is one of the founders of generative semantics and a reference author in the field of metaphors. He has been an adviser to politicians such as the former U.S. President Bill Clinton and the former President Rodríguez Zapatero.

[90] Mark L. Johnson, professor of philosophy at the University of Oregon, known for his contributions to cognitive science and cognitive linguistics

[91] Professor of Speech Studies at the University of Amsterdam and lecturer at Pompeu Fabra University in Barcelona, Teun van Dijk is one of the founders of Critical Discourse Analysis. This is not a method for linguistic analysis but a social movement with an interdisciplinary approach that studies power discourse and the cognitive fixation of beliefs. In more simple terms, it analyses how the dominant elite uses public discourse to fix ideas as the dominant way of thinking and thus subtly gain control over the beliefs of the population.

[92] For an in-depth explanation, see JIMÉNEZ HUERTAS, CARME, *Los orígenes del lenguaje* (2018, in press).

5.3 Toponymy

Toponymy (or geographical onomastics) is the study of the etymology of place names. It is considered to be the archaeology of languages, because old languages become 'fossilized' in toponymy.

If so many errors have occurred in etymology because a direct affiliation with Latin has not been questioned, toponymy deserves a separate book. To date, a word has only been accepted as pre-Roman if it had no equivalent in Latin. Any similarity has been interpreted as Latinization, ignoring any other considerations.

For instance, philologist Joan Coromines[93] believed that the suffix <-à> at the end of the word meant 'town of', and thus CORNELLÀ meant 'town of Cornelius', ROMANYÀ, 'town of Romanus', LLUÇÀ 'town of Lucius', PREIXANA 'town of Priscus', etc. This statement was made without taking into account that there are multiple Cornellà toponyms in Catalan lands (Cornellà del Llobregat, Cornellà del Terri, Cornellà de Conflent...) so it would certainly be a coincidence that so many towns were founded by citizens called Cornelius. As soon as we study the location of these toponyms ending in –LLÀ, we realize that they are places where rivers, mountains, etc. meet. In no case do they refer to an outstanding local personality. Moreover, Coromines did not verify if these presumed Roman-founded towns already existed before the Romans arrived...

Toponyms give their names to geographic accidents, rivers, mountains, valleys, crags, towns, cities. They are not a result of luck nor do they commemorate specific historical events. They are deliberate and descriptive. Literally, they describe the territory. They designate (i.e. they mark and fix) the place they name. They are composed of a combination of lexemes (words) that help us to accurately identify a place, highlighting a pre-eminent topographic feature or singularity, the proximity to a river, its location at the bottom of a valley, at a junction or under a crag.

A proper noun is an old common noun –or the sum of common components– whose inherent semantic features have been lexicalized in order to designate

---

93 Joan Coromines i Vigneaux (1905-1997) was a Catalan philologist and etymologist, author of the *Diccionario crítico etimológico castellano e hispánico* (Castilian and Hispanic Critical Dictionary of Etymology), considered reference work in the study of Romance languages. Coromines was also the author of the monumental *Onomasticon Cataloniae*, an etymological opus that gathers the origin of more than 400,000 ancient and modern place names, published in eight volumes between 1994 and 1997. Another of his reference works is the *Diccionari Etimològic i Complementari de la Llengua Catalana* (Etymological and Complementary Dictionary of the Catalan Language), published between 1980 and 1991, consisting of nine volumes to which a tenth had to be added, with supplements and an index, in 2001.

a particular person or place. It is obvious that the proper name Montserrat in Catalan means *mont* (mountain) + *serrat* (saw form). It is describing the characteristic form of the Catalan mountain. Over time, the toponym (proper place name) has become an anthroponym (a person's proper name), but both have their origin in a common name or, rather, in the sum of significant common elements.

Interestingly, many toponyms that do not seem to make sense in modern languages actually contain the description of the place in an older language used by the inhabitants that occupied the territory in remote times. This means that, when these places were named, the inhabitants designated them in their own language with a name consisting of descriptive components whose meaning is the sum of the parts. This name has survived for centuries and even millennia, being very resistant to overlapping languages, which allows us to reconstruct the map of archaic populations.

Most toponyms have a remote origin that takes us back to the peoples of the Paleolithic. Those human groups knew their surroundings very well, and to survive they needed to be able to express exactly where they were going or where they came from.

Let us look at a specific example. According to the philologist Joan Coromines,[94] when applying the principle of Latinization of our territories, the name Vallirana stems from the Latin VALERIANA.[95] Other etymologies make it come from the Latin name VALERIUS. There is no evidence that valerian abounded in this place or that any pre-eminent Valerian should have visited or founded it. Moreover, it is absurd that humans used these terms to locate a place, since valerian is a deciduous plant and therefore, during part of the year it will not be found. On the other hand, and for an outsider looking for a particular place, it is not very helpful to know that the town was founded by Valerius; however, it would be helpful to know that it is located on the top of a mountain, at the mouth of the river or at the intersection of two valleys.

Therefore, if we apply the comparative method to other place names that carry the components of VALLIRANA, we find the valley of ARAN. In Basque HARAN means valley. According to philologist Núria Garcia Quera,[96] the place name includes the formants: BA (related to 'water'), LL (related to 'joining'), ARAN (the great valley, composed in turn of AN 'big' and AR 'in

---

94 See footnote 88

95 Herbaceous plant used in medicine as an antispasmodic

96 See note 80. Núria Garcia Quera is a philologist specializing in toponymy.

the middle', i.e. a 'valley'), which would give us 'at the joining of waters, in the great valley'. And where is Vallirana? Between mountains, in the valley between the Penyes del Rovira and the Serra Corredera, in which the waters of several tributaries join, at the massif of Garraf. This is the exact description of the valley that crosses the riverbed of Valirana!

Toponyms do not change easily. Although most of the important place-names (cities, large mountains and rivers) have undergone considerable manipulation, in contrast, and as Bernat Mira Tormo[97] has duly noted, there are usually no great modifications in microtoponymy. To analyze microtoponymy and major toponymy, one must have sound knowledge of the territory. However, since it has little historical relevance, microtoponymy has not received the attention of historians or philologists, and therefore these names have often preserved their original old form, which allows us to perform an less adulterated etymology (although it is impossible to avoid being a victim of multiple interpretations).

What do newly settled populations do with toponyms? As soon as they discover them, they tend to either perform a literal translation into their own language or (if the meaning of the place-name formants is too far removed for them) to 'disfigure' them with a phonetic adaptation which means something in the new language, even if this adaptation is quite different from the original meaning. For example: the toponym *La Pera Aguda*, where 'Pera' means *piedra* (stone) + 'aguda' (sharp) has ended up being called 'L'Apareguda' (The Apparition), relating it to a legend that tells of the appearance of a witch.[98]

Aside from these anecdotal cases, it is a verifiable fact that many toponyms are the sum of the formants that describe the topography of the place, and therefore toponymy allows us to rediscover words that have disappeared (or have been de-lexicalized) in modern languages. The matrix language from which the place names were defined was compositional and has reached us at two different levels. On the one hand, we have the phonetic level. There are sound similarities (mostly consonantal) that show surprising, strange relationships, which are unexplained or inexplicable according to official standards. Comparative grammarians have studied these phonetic changes based on the synchronic and diachronic analysis of related languages, which has allowed them to verify the systematic nature of the Consonantal Shift. However, the semantic level has not been studied so far.

---

97 https://vascoiberismo.wordpress.com/

98 Reference taken from BERTRAN, JOSEP M. *Toponímia a l'abast: Introducció a l'estudi dels noms de lloc.* (2013).

Núria Garcia Quera,[99] who has lived in the Pallars Sobirà since 1986, has chosen this region as a test bench for her toponymic studies. Her interest in languages and deep knowledge of the Pyrenees territory helped her to understand that the etymology of toponyms offered an adequate explanation for place names. When she interconnected the syllabic elements of place names with the geographical elements, she discovered that the former were authentic lexemes of an ancient language. However, what is most amazing is that these lexemes are still present in the current lexicon of various Romance and non-Romance languages. The semantic relationship is so obvious that it seems incredible. Let us look at some examples of Pyrenean toponyms formed by joining lexemes that directly refer to this common parent tongue:

> BAR/BOR (Lla**vor**sí, Lla**vo**rre...) we find it in places where there is the mouth of a river. It stems from the union of BA (water) + AR (between) = 'between waters' and is also present in words such as **bar**ca (boat).
>
> ES (**Es**terri, **Es**tós...) is almost always found at the end of a valley. It refers to the idea of a place that has only one exit and gives us many words such as **ex**treme, **ec**centric, **ex**tract. We also find it in '**es**ku' (hand, in Basque), and it is part of words that require using one's hand such as **es**calera (ladder), **es**pada (sword), **es**cribir (writing), etc.
>
> GE/GI (**Ge**rri, Amit**ge**s...) is found where there are geminate geographical elements, such as rocks, meadows, etc. We find this lexeme in words such as **ge**melos (twins), **gi**gante (giant; meaning 'similar, but big'), **ge**nitales (genitals)...
>
> KA (**Ca**dí, Es**ca**rt, Bres**ca**...) is found in places with huge rock walls and appears in words such as ro**ca** (rock), but also in **co**ral, **ca**lcio (calcium), es**ca**rpado (steep)...
>
> LLA (Tora**lla**, **Lla**vorsí...) is found in joining points. We find it in words like co**lla**do (mountain pass), but also in rodi**lla** (knee), tobi**llo** (ankle), ani**llo** (ring), hebi**lla** (buckle), etc.
>
> M is present in elevations (**M**ontsent, **M**almercat, **M**encui...) and therefore it is found in the words **m**ontaña (mountain), **m**onte (hill), **m**ama (breast)...
>
> OL is related to places where there is a turn in the river (Puj**ol**, T**ol**zó...) and we find this lexeme in a multitude of words containing the idea of something curved or circular: s**ol** (sun), círcu**lo** (circle), **oll**a (pot), **ol**a (wave), **ol**iva (olive), per**ol** (casserole)...

---

99 See footnote 80

RRE / RRI (Este**rri**, Ge**rri**, **Ri**alp...) is found in the plain lands by the riverside, which were possibly grasslands that were flooded periodically from annual floods. This lexeme is found in *río* (river), *ri*ego (irrigation), *ri*ba (riverbank)...

TA/TE (Es**ta**ron, Por**tar**ró, Broa**te**...) is in places of obliged passage, such as mountain passes. It contains the idea of *puerta* (door).

TOR (**Tor**ena, **Tor**la, **Tor**nafort...) is a 'not very high elevation', in Catalan *turó* (hill). The idea of a small elevation that can be bypassed gives us words like **tor**re (tower), **tor**tuga (turtle), **tor**no (lathe) or **tor**so (trunk).

UI (Bern**ui**, Embon**ui**, Menc**ui**, Arest**ui**...) is always in strategic places, with a great panoramic view. In Catalan eye is *ull*, pronounced *ui* in different places. The villages that carry UI were vantage points, they were the 'eyes' of the mountains. This lexeme is found in words like **vi**gía (watcher), **vi**gilar (to watch), **vi**dente (seer)...

This similarity in the formants leads us to consider the same compositional structure for common nouns and proper nouns – which allows us to assert that formants, now semantically bleached, come from ancient lexemes.

Why? Because many of these formants have survived in the modern languages. For example, the word *bassa* (pond) in Catalan (and *balsa* in Spanish) consists of BA *agua* (water) and SA *contenedor* (container), which leads us to the definition found in the dictionary of the Royal Spanish Academy: a hollow in the ground that is filled with water, either naturally or artificially. *Bassa*, then, is a 'water container'. What happens then with the word *carbassa* (*calabaza*, in Spanish; pumpkin, in English)?

Having established that the lexeme C+vocal+R refers to 'something hard and external' *corteza* (bark), *cartón* (cardboard), *coraza* (shell), *corcho* (cork)..., *carbassa* would then be 'hard water container'. Note that, in many areas in the world (such as Africa, Asia), this is still the main use given to pumpkins.

Thus, the derivation is only apparent: the new words arise from the sum of significant elements that seem to refer to a metalanguage formed by related ideas or concepts that go beyond words, as explained here in the chapter on etymology and as further elaborated in the chapters on morphosyntax.

Now I would like to speak about Basque a little. As it has been noted so far, it is the only language on the Iberian Peninsula –and one of the few European languages– that is not part of the Indo-European family. It is considered a typologically agglutinative and genetically isolated language. Due to its characteristics, in Basque it is very easy to create new words by using the composition method. Let us look at an example:

eye = begi

hair = ile

skin = azal

eyelash = betile = be (eye) + (t) + ile (hair) = hair of the eye

eyelid = betazalen = be (eye) + (t) + azal = skin of the eye[100]

What is interesting here? This compositional method seems to provide the basis for many Spanish words. Here is another example:

etxe = house

etxe (house) bola (round) = etxola = Spanish *chabola* (shack)

etxe (house) alea (grande) = Spanish *chalé* (cottage, chalet)

etxe (house) hotza (cold) = Spanish *choza* (hut)

etxe (house) ona (good) = etxona = Spanish *casona* (large house, mansion)[101]

Ancient Basque did not leave any writing, nor does it correspond to any creed or religion This is why it was never a language associated with power institutions.

The Jesuit Manuel de Larramendi wrote an apology for Basque, defending it as the language of the substrate that had given rise to many Spanish words. Moreover, he praised it for being a philosophical language. His most important work was the *Diccionario trilingüe castellano, bascuence y latín* (*Trilingual Dictionary of Spanish, Basque and Latin*) (1745), which marks the beginning of linguistic studies of Basque. Another advocate of the perfection and antiquity of the Basque language was Pablo Pedro de Astarloa, who published his *Apología de la lengua vascongada. Un ensayo critico filosófico de su perfección y antigüedad sobre todas las que se conocen.* (*Apology for the Basque language. A critical and philosophical essay on its perfection and antiquity over all the other known languages*) in 1803. According to Astarloa, in Basque, each syllable and each letter had its own meaning.

---

100 Examples provided by Xebe Diaz Zumalabe (2013)

101 Examples provided by Pako Iriarte Arruti (2014)

Many subsequent authors have defended the antiquity of Basque.[102] Going one step further, the German linguist Wilhelm von Humboldt claimed that the Iberian language was the ancestor of Basque. In two of his works, Humboldt argues that it is possible to recognize Basque in the toponymy (names of mountains, rivers, rocks, valleys and villages) throughout Europe.[103]

Let us return to Romance languages: researcher Lucian Iosif Cueşdean claims that Romanian is the oldest language in Europe;[104] studying Romanian, he has come to conclusions that are similar to those presented in this book: the ancient language was based on significant units (which he calls morphemes). I consider these to be lexemes, as they have full meaning.

For all these reasons, the parent tongue from which the Romances derive would be the language spoken in the Paleolithic era in Europe, in Mediterranean and other territories. Linguistic similarities respond to the symbolic value of formants that, following an identical process of composition, laid the foundations for many languages. On the other hand, divergences appeared with sedentarism, during the Neolithic period. In this process, Latin was one of many Romance languages and not the parent tongue.

The hypothesis regarding etymology and toponymy presented in this book seriously questions the received theory of the evolution of Romance languages and of their affiliation with Latin. If Romance languages were derived from Latin, it is difficult to understand why they did not copy the rich and precise system of conjunctions from Classical Latin. However, it is an indisputable fact that the basic grammatical particles of Latin are not found in the Romances. We have no trace of structures introduced by Latin conjunctions: *ac, an, at, autem, cum, donec, enim, ergo, etiam, etsi, haud, igitur, ita, nam, postquam, quidem, sed, ut, utrum,* and *vel.*

All of this will be noted in greater detail when analysing the morphosyntax.

---

102 Luis Pericot, Louis Charpentier, Julio Caro Baroja, etc.

103 Other advocates of Basque-Europeanism are Theo Vennemann, Alberto Porlan, Félix Zubiaga, Josu Naberan and Javier Goitia.

104 CUEŞDEAN, LUCIAN IOSIF. *Româna, limba vechii Europe*. Editura Solif. Bucharest (2006).

CHAPTER 6

6.1 Morphosyntax

If in previous chapters we have put forward many reasons to support the hypothesis that Romance languages neither derive from Latin nor can they be related through filiation, when we enter the fields of morphology and syntax the reasons acquire such magnitude that they become overwhelming. Gone are the morphemes and nexuses establishing syntactic correlations. There is no continuity: on the contrary, there is a real break, which is explained as a regression. And yet this 'setback' is simultaneous in all Romances. When the Empire collapsed, how is it possible that the solutions converged?

In historical grammar it is explained that Vulgar Latin 'lost' grammatical elements and went back to a parataxis, i.e. returned to the primitive state of a language that uses simple sentences or elemental composition by coordination or juxtaposition. The regression was of such a magnitude that speakers had to resort to non-verbal language or gestures in order to understand each other. It took centuries to achieve hypotaxis again, which is the state of development of a language that allows any kind of inter-sentence relationship. This is explained quite earnestly in the textbooks of schools and universities: no thought is given to the fact that what is being described is oral language based on records written in another language, in this case Latin, a dead language that nobody spoke and therefore was little known and poorly written. To say that speakers stopped using grammatical resources would be almost like arguing that English, which has no subjunctive mode, cannot form subordinate sentences...[105]

Sometimes it is not easy to establish a separation between phonetics, morphology and syntax, because morphemes can consist of a single phoneme that gives us the syntactic information. Therefore, when we are told that it was the loss of final consonants (apocope) that affected the morphemic system providing all the syntactic information (declensions), to the point of forcing the language to radically change the way the relationship between words was defined, we are overcome by a sort of existential despair

---

[105] English currently has a function as an international lingua franca just like Latin had in its day. It is learned as a second language, hence and the level of mastery can vary considerably. For some people it is sometimes very frustrating to spend years studying English without seeing results. Writing it incorrectly and not knowing how to use *modal verbs* properly does not mean that there is a Vulgar English; it just shows us that the speaker lacks the skill to properly structure a language that is not their own. This is exactly the same as what we find in the texts written in Medieval Latin.

just by imagining the chaos that speakers of so-called Vulgar Latin must have suffered... and that supposedly lasted four centuries!

As we have tried to show throughout this book, languages do not work that way. Basic information that entails semantic confusion cannot be 'lost'. If speakers were so worried because the elimination of geminate consonants had originated a growing number of voiceless stops and decided to voice them... if it were true that voiced consonants became closer, and that from all this effort that exceeds any ordinary citizen's grammatical knowledge it turned out that, IN MEDIAS RES, consonants ended up disappearing and creating a real confusion when case endings were dropped... – how frustrating must that have been! It would have been a complete waste of time! Of course it is a difficult argument to defend, because nobody would favour a tendency that creates such confusion!

It is much more plausible, however, that things must have happened the other way around. The devoicing or disappearance of case endings could only take place in a language in which opposition was not necessary, otherwise they would have been preserved, as in German or Greek, where nouns are still declined. In these chapters devoted to morphosyntax, we will see that, according to the linguistic universals established by Greenberg,[106] Latin and Romance languages belong to different linguistic typologies. The order of the constituents of the sentence marks the textual typology of the languages, so it is not something that can be easily modified. The possible patterns of variation are very limited.

Historical grammar books indicate that linguistic change in morphology is produced by analogy, since the tendency to suppress unproductive or less used systems acts as an instigating model. We are told that, in this way, we tend to use a single regular model. However, experience shows us that the opposite is true: the more a verb is used, the more likely it is to have an irregular paradigm, so it can hardly act as an instigator. Thus, we can see that the Spanish verb *ir* and its equivalents in Catalan *anar*, French *aller* and English *to go*, are irregular verbs in all these languages. The same thing happens with the verbs *ser/estar* (to be) and *haber* (to have). An example of this is the list of irregular verbs that one must memorize when studying English, because they are the most used and the formation of their past and past participle does not follow a pattern that can be justified by the principle of analogy. Moreover, Chomskyan grammar has identified as 'impossible'

---

106 American linguist Joseph Greenberg (1915-2001) is known for his work on linguistic classification and typology. From a sample of 30 languages, he established a set of 45 basic linguistic universals.

many sentences with similar structures, which should be possible if they only depended on analogy. At some level, there is a principle of selective blocking that marks possible and impossible relations between grammatical elements. This means that analogy is not the engine of language acquisition.

Another aspect, already pointed out when talking about stress, is the preservation of the main stress in compound words. This feature could be the result of an agglutinative or compositional language substrate that would form new words by adding significant elements. This would explain why Latin's casual inflective system did not succeed; and why it has this surprising tendency to use periphrases, which cannot be explained by the Principle of Linguistic Economy.

Let us analyse, very briefly, the characteristics that we find in Latin and in the Romances regarding the different grammatical categories, their form and formation (morphology) and their function within the sentence (syntax). I will now focus on the differences that separate the Romances from Latin.

6.2 Morphological generalities in inflected forms

Some of the characteristics of the Romances that diverge from Latin are:

- In the Romances, there is a proliferation of composition with the addition of suffixes, sometimes repetitively;
- The morphology of Latin has a synthetic tendency: words are inflected with endings (case morphemes that are added to the root) that provide all the morphosyntactic information. Latin therefore has an inflected morphology that creates a nominal (declensions) and verbal (conjugations) paradigm;
- Romance languages prefer analytic constructions. The nominal paradigm is reduced to the grammatical number and does not present any case differentiation. The syntactic function is indicated by:
  - The use of independent particles (prepositions, conjunctions)
  - Concordance:
    - Concordance in number and person between subject and verb;
    - Concordance in gender and number between article or determiner, adjective and noun; and
  - A fixed order of constituents.

- The verbal paradigm of the Romances is similar but with some substantial differences from Latin: preferential use of compound tenses, periphrasis, locutions...

Languages are studied and classified based on their morphology, i.e. the processes used to create new words. Linguists recognize five basic morphological types:

- Isolating or analytic languages: words are invariable and the syntactic relationship is established based on the word order (for example, Chinese and Vietnamese);
- Agglutinative languages: words are formed by a sum or sequence of morphs,[107] each one bringing part of the meaning (for example, Turkish and Swahili);
- Inflected languages: words are considered lexemes, to which terminations or affixes are added to express new meanings or morphosyntactic properties. They are also called synthetic languages because the union of suffixes synthesizes information into a single word. It is not a two-way relationship because there are many more lexemes (the root that carries the meaning) than morphemes (elements that add morphosyntactic information) (for example, Latin and Greek);
- Incorporating or polysynthetic languages: they can synthesize whole sentences in a single word by agglutination and inflection (for example, some Amerindian and Indigenous Australian languages); and
- Languages with infixes: languages that can include morphological elements within them (for example, Arabic and Hebrew).

The Romances are considered to be inflected languages. Hence, the lexeme of the word carries the greatest semantic weight, nuanced by the addition of affixes.

Two types of affixes are distinguished: inflectional affixes, and derivational affixes.

Inflectional affixes provide the morphological information of nominal and verbal inflection. There are nominal morphemes of gender and number, and verbal morphemes of person, number, tense, mode and aspect. This process is known as suffixation.

---

107 A morpheme is the minimum unit of grammatical analysis with recognized phonological, morphological, syntactic and semantic value. A morph is the sound expression of a morpheme, for example morph [-n] in "*cantaban*" is the expression of the morpheme in the third person plural.

However, in addition to the nominal and verbal inflection already mentioned, inflected languages use two processes for the creation of new words: derivation and composition.

Derivation forms new words by joining derivational affixes (prefixes, infixes or suffixes) to a lexical basis. This process is very productive, because new words can be created for everything the language needs to express out of a limited number of derivational affixes. This process is a feature of all languages and is applied naturally. However, today it has been standardized by the linguistic institutions that are in charge of accepting and determining the incorporation of new terms (neologisms).

Composition is the morphological process by which new words are formed by joining two or more already existing words. Words in the same category can be joined: for instance, two nouns (*landowner*), two adjectives (*bittersweet*), or words of different categories such as an adjective and a noun (*smartphone*), a verb and a noun (*spreadsheet*), etc.

Below I will review the characteristics of derivational affixes:

- Most affixes are stressed and impose the main stress on the new word. Suffixation moves the stress to the right, so *débil* (weak), with the stress in the penultimate syllable, becomes *debilidad* (weakness), with the stress on the last syllable. In prefixation, if the affix is stressed it does not displace the main stress. Instead, a secondary stress is usually generated on the prefix: *extraordinario* (extraordinary).

- Suffixes have another very interesting ability: they modify the grammatical category. Thus for example the affix *–dor* (in English *–er*) changes a verb into a noun. It means an agent that performs an action: *trabajar > trabajador* (to work > worker); or, the place where something is performed: *mirar > mirador* (to look; viewpoint); or, the instrument with which something is performed *colar > colador* (to strain > strainer). Another example that changes a noun into an adjective is the affix *–oso* (in English *–ous*), which means a common characteristic, attribute or tendency of something. So, from *amistad* we have *amistoso* (friendship; friendly); from *bosque, boscoso* (forest; woody). The affix *–ble* has the function of converting verbs (that is, actions) into adjectives (that is, the capacity or characteristic to perform that action), and thus what can be counted (which is an action) is *countable*; what can be measured, *measurable*; what can be believed, *believable*.

Affixes can be joined in series that create new words in a different grammatical category and with a different meaning within the same paradigm. Let us look at an example:

Norma	Noun	Lexeme or root
Normal (norm + al)	adjective	If the affix <-al>, which means 'quality of', is added to the noun *norma*, an adjective *normal* is obtained. Therefore, the affix <-al> converts nouns into adjectives.
Normalmente (normal + mente)	adverb	If the lexical affix <-mente> is added to the adjective *normal*, an adverb is obtained.
Normalizar (normal + iz + ar)	verb	If the infix <-itz-, -iz->, which contains a plural semantic nuance, is added to the adjective *normal*, the quality of normal encompasses more objects and persons. This infix converts adjectives into verbs.

What information does this table offer us? There is a model of the internal way a language works, which follows derivative parameters, which in turn determine the grammatical categories. Out of a few lexemes that a speaker knows and a limited number of affixes, new words of different categories are created. On the other hand, words have a Thematic Relation that governs the associated role of each of the complements (syntagmatic elements).

For instance, at the phonological level, the morpheme <-ismo> is formed by the morph [ismo]; at the morphological level, it is a derivational affix; at the syntactic level, it creates abstract nouns (such as *cristianismo*, *naturalismo*); and at the semantic level it has the meaning of movement or doctrine relative to the noun it accompanies.

However, not all morphemes are so transparent. For example, the affix <-a->, which in Spanish at the morphological level indicates that a verb belongs to the first conjugation, has apparently no syntactic or semantic value.[108] The same could be said about the infix < -iz- -itz>, previously mentioned in *normalizar*. And yet, the infix <-iz -itz> exists in Basque. For example, the verb

---

108 Although the origin of verbal conjugations is unknown, there are indications that, thousands of years ago, thematic vowels contributed to classifying verbs semantically.

IZAN with a plural object takes the infix <-it->, and the third person of the plural also takes a <-z->. Is this a coincidence?

In philology studies, the properties of derivational affixes are considered arbitrary. Derivative morphology is based on joining a derivational morpheme (affix) with a noun or lexeme that gives it its semantic nuance (root). Therefore, the parts or segments that add the grammatical information have been interpreted as grammatical marks whose meaning depends on the lexeme they accompany.

The way in which the speakers of a language apply these mechanisms for creating new words through derivation remains a mystery. These internal rules are applied without the need to learn them consciously. If the basis of the process were analogy, we would create new words at random and the result could be chaotic. However, speakers do not make mistakes. For example, they know that from the adjective *largo* one can create an action, **a***largar* (long; lengthen); from *grande*, **a***grandar* (large, enlarge); from *blando*, **a***blandar* (soft; soften). On the other hand, the action of *ancho* is **ens***anchar* (width; widen), and not 'anchar'. Why is it not possible to create an action such as 'anchar' or '**em**blandar'? Likewise, when we want to confine something, in a real or metaphorical sense, we can **en***cajonar*, from *cajón* (drawer); **en***sobrar*, from *sobre* (envelope); **en***cestar* from *cesta* (basket); **em***botellar* from *botella* (bottle); **en***casillar* from *casilla* (box) but we cannot '**en**ollar' from *olla* (pot). There is a very deep semantic barrier here, which all speakers know and acknowledge... even children.

There is another aspect I would like to discuss here. Derivational suffixes exceed a hundred by far and, aside from being very productive, they add significant nuances such as actions, results of actions, collective nouns, jobs, diminutives, augmentatives, tendencies, attitudes, etc. As previously discussed, they also have the ability to change the grammatical category of words. All this makes us consider that these are old lexical morphemes coming from an old compositional or agglutinative language. Over time and by repeated use, we have 'forgotten' that these affixes have a meaning and we have lexicalized the new derived words as if they were independent units, when in fact they are made up of compositional formants. In support of this hypothesis, affixes are stressed and can displace the main stress, the grammatical category or even the gender of the word, if it is a noun.

New studies try to investigate these changes in the reverse and thus retrace their ancient roots. American linguist Joan ByBee[109] has studied the recurring properties of morphological systems, describing correlations between meaning and form. This has also been studied for French, by Danielle Corbin.[110] For Romanian, Mihai Vinereanu[111] has published an etymological dictionary where he questions the Roman origin of Romanian and advocates for the native origin of 85% of lexical elements.

This compositional character is also found in Basque, as previously noted here when speaking of etymology and toponymy.

And finally, it seems that the nature of the Iberian language was also compositional.

Why has this subject not been further studied? Because it has been accepted without challenge that everything that matched, or could more or less be approximated to match, Latin must have derived from Latin. And when it was different, historical linguists have tried to explain its evolution through successive changes, as the result of a degradation suffered by Vulgar Latin.

When languages share the same mechanisms, the results should be similar. To understand how changes occur, we must examine these patterns. A pattern shared by Romance languages should be identifiable on this evolutionary path and be part of the Latin language. However, that is not what we find.

Whatever the parent tongue from which the Romances stem, it should have a strong compositional character. When we decide to connect the 'fossilized' morphology in today's vocabulary with ancient languages that existed prior to the so-called Romanization, then will we be able to identify more precisely where Romance languages come from.

Let us now focus on the morphological characteristics of the nominal forms.

6.3 Nouns

Some of the characteristics of the nouns that diverge from Latin are:

- Absence of declinations.

---

109 BYBEE, JOAN. *Morphology. A Study of the Relation between Meaning and Form*. Typological Studies in Languages, vol. 9. John Benjamin Publishing, Amsterdam (1985).

110 CORBIN, D. *Morphologie dérivationnelle et du lexique structuration*. Tubingen. Vols 1 and 2 (1987).

111 VINEREANU, MIHAI. *Dicționar etimologic al limbii române pe baza cercetărilor de indo-europenistică*. Bucharest: Alcor Edimpex (2008).

- Presence of prepositions for grammatical functions.
- Uniqueness in forming the plural.
- Absence of neuter gender.

As mentioned above, historical grammar has so far explained that it was phonetic change which provoked the loss of casual suffixes. Initially, there was a decrease in the number of forms differentiated, and the number of cases went from five to three (nominative, accusative-ablative, genitive-dative). In ancient French and Catalan (12th and -13th Centuries), an opposition of two cases (straight/oblique) has been found, and some Romansch varieties maintained the remainders of the declension until the 18th Century. Finally, most Romance languages completely disregarded Latin declensions and now only Romanian retains case oppositions... Or perhaps we should put this information into context?

It is usually stated that Romanian nouns have inflected forms with case marks for nominative (S, subject), accusative (DO, direct object), genitive (GC, genitive construction) and dative (IO, indirect object). There is also a vocative case, which is used to address people directly. In nouns, nominative and accusative have identical forms; so do genitive and dative. Experts say that Romanian cases were inherited from Latin, and use this as proof of the existence of Vulgar Latin. However, things are a little more complicated, because the inflection actually belongs to the article, not the noun. Unlike Spanish, the definite article in Romanian is placed after and not before the noun. And this is the article that presents a case inflection. Thus, if Latin had no articles, how can this case inflection be a Latin heritage?

The article is a grammatical category that did not exist in Latin. Its position after the noun is also very important, because it completely changes the explanations of the origin and evolution of the nominal inflection in the Romances through a theoretical Vulgar Latin. But we must also add the presence of prepositions to mark grammatical functions, which mysteriously brings Romanian closer to other Romance languages and reduces the 'need' for nominal case markings.

To put it very simply, in Romanian the direct object is marked with the preposition *pe* (to), while circumstantial functions are marked with *pe* (on), *în* (in, into), *la* (to, toward), *din* (in, from), *cu* (with,) *fără* (without), *lângă* (near), *sub* (under), *despre* (about). Genitive syntagma present the same order as in other Romances, i.e. Noun + Genitive, with the case marked through the article of the determiner in genitive. This definitively distances Romanian from Latin and brings it closer to the rest of Romance languages.

What significance does the Romances' non-use of the grammatical case system to mark syntactic functions really have? Is this indeed a degradation of Vulgar Latin? Perhaps we might find an explanation in Iberian. Quoting Orduña,[112] there are data that allow us to defend the view that Iberian was an ergative language, with no specific marks to distinguish between subject and object. The agent would instead be marked with the suffix <-ka>.[113] Were it possible to prove this feature, there would be an explanation consistent with the absence of grammatical cases in peninsular Romance languages that were formed from Iberian, thereby distancing them from Latin.[114]

Regarding the number, in Latin the plural varied according to each declension. In the Western Romances, the marking of plural is the suffix <-s>. However, south and east of La Spezia-Rimini line, the distinction is made by changing the final vowel i/e, as in contemporary Italian and Romanian. There is therefore uniqueness in the adopted solutions.

A note regarding Basque: it forms the plural in -k. Hungarian does too: *ember* (man) —*emberek* (men).

With regards to the gender, Latin had three genders: feminine, masculine and neuter.

Western Romance languages only have the masculine-feminine opposition. Only articles and third person pronouns have a form for neuter.[115]

Romanian has neuter nouns. However, unlike Latin, the Romanian neuter gender does not have forms of its own but encompasses words that in singular behave as masculine and in plural as feminine. Therefore, it would not be a neuter gender but rather an ambiguous gender whose inflection changes gender, using masculine forms for singular and feminine for plural.

---

112 ORDUÑA, EDUARDO. *Ergatividad en ibérico*. Revista de Lingüística y Filología Clásica LXXVI 2 (2008), pp. 275-302.

113 Since Iberian script is syllabic, we can find the phoneme [k] represented using different graphemes when it is attached to different vowels, such as <a, e, i>.

114 Latin is an accusative language that encompasses the subject and the agent in the nominative function and, on the other hand, marks the object in the accusative.

115 Some authors argue that the neuter gender in Spanish is not exactly a grammatical gender as such but rather it is used to designate certain abstract notions. These would include the article: *lo*; personal pronouns: *ello, lo*; demonstrative pronouns: *esto, eso, aquello*; indefinite pronouns: *algo, nada*; quantifying adverbs: *cuanto, tanto*.

The neuter gender also exists in Greek, German and Russian.

There is no grammatical gender distinction in Basque. Neither is there one in English.

6.4 Adjectives
Some of the characteristics of the adjectives that diverge from Latin are:

- As a rule, the adjective follows the noun in all Romances. We will look at this topic again when discussing syntax.
- There is a substitution of the analytical comparative and superlative forms of adjectives with a periphrastic structure.

The synthetic comparative and superlative of Latin (also present in other Indo-European languages, such as English) do not exist in Romance languages. The latter use an analytical construction for both, following the model: *is more X than*, or *the most X of*.

Only the synthetic comparisons *mejor* (best), *peor* (worst), *mayor* (major), *menor* (minor), and some learned words such as *óptimo* (optimal) and *pésimo* (extremely badly), are preserved.

The absolute superlative is formed synthetically by adding the suffix *-ísimo* to the root of the qualifying adjective. Although generally almost all adjectives can be formed synthetically, there are some that are irregular or only for literary use. When speaking, the periphrasis adding the adverb of quantity *muy X* (very X) is the most frequently used construction.

6.5 Pronouns
Some of the characteristics of the pronouns that diverge from Latin are:

- Incorporation of prepositions.
- Increased number of forms: unstressed (clitic) pronouns.
- *hi* and *en* pronouns.
- Distinction between informal and formal address (*tuteo* and *voseo*).

Latin pronouns were declined and not accompanied by a preposition. All Romances agree on incorporating prepositions into the stressed forms of pronouns to indicate its syntactic function.

One of the main differences from Latin is the wide diversity of pronominal forms according to whether they are stressed or unstressed. In the Romances, when unstressed pronouns do not have a preposition, they are used as a verbal complement that can take the clitic form, i.e. they are pronounced connected to the verb. They can be proclitic (forms that precede the verb) or enclitic (forms that go after the verb):

- Their placement in front of or behind the verb is not arbitrary but subject to rules.
- The same verb can have two or even three clitic pronouns, which precede or follow the verb, always as a block.
- The order is not free and is subject to the rules: DO + IO + VC or PrepO[116].
- Enclitic pronouns may or may not be graphically attached to the verb they accompany, according to the verb tense and varying in the different Romance languages.

In Spanish pronouns are written as a single word when they follow the infinitive, the gerund, the imperative and the present subjunctive. In Catalan and French, vowel elisions allow a much more extensive use of the enclitics, as they have a wide variety of elided forms.

Morphologically, the pronouns of Romance languages show identical morphemes such as —m— for the first person singular, —t— for the second person singular, —l— for the third person, —n— for the first person plural and —v— for the second person plural.

In Romanian,[117] personal pronouns also show an enormous diversity of stressed and unstressed pronominal forms that did not exist in Latin and which, strangely enough, closely resemble Galician and Catalan. For example, the stressed personal pronoun of the first person 'eu'[118] is identical in Romanian and Galician. How is this possible, if there has been no contact between these languages for two thousand years?

---

[116] DO direct object; IO indirect object; VC verbal complement or PrepO prepositional object.

[117] The Romanian language has a long list of clitic elements: there are pronominal, adverbial clitics, prepositions and even some auxiliary verbs that, when coming into contact with vowels, produce elisions, contractions or diphthongs. The graphical mark used to indicate formal changes is the hyphen (-).

[118] The pronoun 'eu' is pronounced 'yeu' in the south, and 'yo' in the rest of the country (Mihaela Alda).

Personal pronouns in Romanian. Stressed forms

	first person		second person		third person	
	singular	plural	singular	plural	singular	plural
N	eu	noi	tu	voi	el/ea	ei/ele
Ac	mine	noi	tine	voi	el/ea/sine	ei/ele/sine
D	mie	nouă	ție	vouă	lui/ei	lor
G	-	-	-	-	lui/ei	lor

Following is a table with the unstressed personal pronouns of Romanian:

Personal pronouns in Romanian. Unstressed forms

	first person		second person		third person	
	singular	plural	singular	plural	singular	plural
N	-	-	-	-	-	-
Ac	mă	ne	te	vă	îl/o	îi/le
D	îmi	ne	îți	vă	îi	le
G	-	-	-	-	-	-

Unstressed forms for the accusative can have multiple subforms, depending on whether they are placed in front of or behind the verb, or whether they are combined with other clitics.

Personal pronouns in Romanian. Unstressed forms in the accusative

first person		second person		third person	
singular	plural	singular	plural	singular	plural
mă	ne	te	vă	masculine îl; -l, l-, -l-	masculine îi; -i, i-, -i-
-mă, mă-	-ne, ne-	-te, te-	-vă, vă-	feminine o:	feminine le;
m-, -m-	-ne-	-te-	v-, -v-	-o, o-, -o-	-le, le-, -le-

This complex clitic system is very similar to Catalan: in fact, if we want to offer a logical explanation that fits in with the evolutionist theories stemming from Latin, they look too similar. Only 'o' is different in the feminine accusative, since in Catalan, but especially in Spanish, the morpheme 'o' is usually identified with the masculine. Pronominal forms in Catalan are one of its most genuine and complex characteristics, and have been the object of many studies. In his doctoral thesis, Pau Maré i Soler[119] noted the resemblance between the Romanian feminine morpheme 'o' and the Catalan neuter enclitic pronoun 'ho'. He has also studied the learning contexts of Catalan by Romanians, as well as the variables of the clitic pronouns in Romanian and in Catalan.

Another characteristic of Catalan is the existence of two pronominal particles, *en* and *hi*, that are used in the pronominal substitution of a prepositional object or an indefinite syntagma.

- The *en* pronoun replaces an indefinite noun syntagma, taking the function of a direct object or a prepositional object when introduced by the preposition *de* (from).
- The *hi* pronoun replaces a noun syntagma taking the function of a prepositional object when introduced by the prepositions /*a, en, amb, per*/ (to, in, with, for). It also replaces verb complements (adverbial and prepositional syntagmas) and the predicative adjective complement.

In expressions that indicate movement, these pronouns are used very frequently to substitute place names: *Vaig a Barcelona > jo hi vaig* (in English: I go to Barcelona > *I go). And in changing direction: *Vinc de Barcelona > jo en vinc* (in English: I come from Barcelona > *I come).

These pronouns do not exist in Latin and are untranslatable into Spanish and into English. However, we find them in French. There is also a similar correspondent in Greek.

Voseo, or formal address, is used to show courtesy or respect. It has been documented since ancient times, in the 4th Century AD, and presents alternations between pronouns and verbal forms. It consists of replacing the *tuteo* (or informal pronoun) for the second person singular (*tú*) with a formula of respect, as if it were the third person singular (*usted*) or the second person plural (*vos*).

The forms of address have been changing throughout history and their use varied across countries. In Spain, the pronoun *usted* is now commonly used as a courtesy form and to address strangers. It must be repeated much more frequently, because its use with the verbal forms of the third person creates a semantic ambiguity with regard to the referent. In Spain, the pronoun *vos* is reserved for formal events. In Catalan, it has a very restricted use as it is

---

119 MARÉ I SOLER, PAU. *L'ús dels clítics pronominals del català i la seva adquisició per parlants de romanès i de tagal.* Universitat de Girona (2011). Can be viewed online at:
http://www.tdx.cat/bitstream/handle/10803/69939/tpms.pdf;jsessionid=9A85006534D-4564C9443ECC6347AC17D.tdx1?sequence=2

reserved for occasions that do not require a distinction between singular and plural, i.e. when the recipient is unknown. On the contrary, in Hispanic American countries, the *voseo* is very widespread and widely used. It presents different forms and uses, depending on the country, and it affects verb conjugations. The pronoun *vos* coexists as a familiar form, and *usted* is the polite form.

In Romanian there are many courtesy pronouns. Unlike any other Romance language, Romanian pronouns indicate three different degrees of intimacy with the interlocutor:

- *tu/voi* (you); *el, ea/ei, ele* (he/ she/ they) and also *dânsul, dânsa/dânşii, dânsele* in Moldavia (and in academic Romanian), the latter are used as personal pronouns, while in the dialects of Transylvania they have a touch of courtesy.[120]

- *dumneata* (you, polite singular)/*dumneavoastră* (you, polite plural); *dumnealui, dumneaei / dumnealor* (courtesy pronouns for the third person, non-existent in other Romances): they are used for relatives and elders.

- d*umneavoastră* (you, formal) - used for a single person, denotes a higher degree of courtesy.

Most of these forms are compound words with 'domnia' (grace) and a possessive determiner, just as in Spanish. Also, in Romanian there are a lot of pronominal phrases such as 'domnia ta', 'domnia sa', 'domniile lor', etc. which literally mean 'your grace', 'his grace', 'their graces'. They are forms of protocol use.

The distinction between *tuteo* and *voseo*, so frequent in the Romances, was inexistent in Latin, where there were no courtesy pronouns. Nor does English have this distinctive treatment.

6.6 Determiners

The characteristics of the determiners that diverge from Latin are:

- Reduction and restructuring of demonstrative pronouns.
- Use of the definite and indefinite article.

---

[120] Verbal forms are used in the plural rather than the singular, to express courtesy. However, this does not apply to the pronoun 'voi'; the subject of these verbal forms will always be 'dumneavoastră'. For example: 'Dumneavoastră vreți...' would be translated literally by 'Your grace would like...', whether it refers to one person or more (Mihaela Alda).

Latin had a large inventory of demonstratives. There were the deictics, which relate the message to the circumstances of the statement, equivalent to our 'this' and 'that'. There were also grammatical and identity demonstratives, used to refer to objects or people mentioned earlier in the speech, either to relate them to their antecedent or to oppose them to others that were different from those mentioned. Spanish and French maintain three distal and proximal demonstratives (*este, ese, aquel*). Catalan also has three forms (*aquest, aqueix, aquell*) but the use of the medial demonstrative is recessive. In Italian (*questo, quello*) and in Romanian (*acest, acel*), a binary system is used, like in English (this, that). For the rest of deictic functions, the Romances use pronouns.

Latin had no articles: neither definite such as in the Spanish *el, la, los, las, lo* (in English: the), or indefinite such as in *un, una, unos, unas* (in English: a, some). However, the article is present in all Romance languages. The use of the definite article is more frequent in French, followed by Catalan and to a lesser extent Spanish, which tends to replace it with a possessive or to eliminate it.

castellano	catalán	
*Ha venido **mi** padre*	*Ha vingut **el** pare*	(**My** *father has come*)
*Graduamos **sus** gafas*	*Li graduem **les** ulleres*	(*We test **your** glasses*)
Conozco a Marta	*Conec **la** Marta*	(*I know Mary*)

While most modern Romance languages place the article before the noun, Romanian places it after, to the right of the noun, for example *lupul* (*the wolf*) and *băiatul* (*the boy*). It is the article that marks the grammatical inflection of the case.

Let's see an example of the article paradigm in Romanian, with *om* (man, masculine) *mamă* (mother, feminine) and *scaun* (chair, neuter):

	Masculine (man)		Feminine (mother)		Neuter (chair)	
	singular	plural	singular	plural	singular	plural
N-Ac	om(u)**l**	oamen**ii**	mama	mam**ele**	scaun(u)**l**	scaun**ele**
D-G	om(u)**lui**	oamen**ilor**	mam**ei**	mam**elor**	scaun(u)**lui**	scaun**elor**
V	om(u)**le**	oamen**ilor**	mam**o**	mam**elor**	-	-

Placing the article to the right of the noun might seem an isolated feature of Romanian. However, it is not the only case.

Recent research carried out with philologist Núria García Quera shows that, in modern languages, these constructions have survived in a fossilized way. By losing the notion that this final particle was the article, it was duplicated to the left. Let's explain it in a little more detail.

As we mentioned when discussing toponymy, the formant L/LL meant 'union or joint', so in Spanish we find it in words related to this meaning: *anilla* (ring), *collar* (necklace), *tobillo* (ankle), *rodilla* (knee)...

It is usually accepted that this affix gives a certain collective sense: we see it in words such as *clientela* (clientele), *personal* (staff), *dineral* (fortune) – which refer to a certain group of customers, people and, respectively, money. But this sense of group is also present in words such as *cuadrilla* (quadrille), *escuela* (school), *muralla* (wall), *metralla* (shrapnel), *morralla* (whitebait), *plantilla* (staff), etc.

Perhaps because of metonymy, the formant L/LL acquired the meaning of collective, something 'related to'. And this meaning is preserved in Catalan better than in Spanish. The Catalan word *mamella* (breast) means 'related to the *mama*' (mother); *cruïlla* (crossing), means 'related to the *creu*' (cross); *davantal* (apron) means 'related to the *davant*' (front); *palmell* (palm of the hand) means 'related to the *palm*'...

However, over time, the meaning of the formants was progressively lost, perhaps because in other contexts it moved away from its original meaning and went unnoticed. Or perhaps also because there is a widespread idea that the Romances are derivational and not compositional, so there is a tendency to omit other considerations.

As a paradigmatic example, let us look at the cases of *villa/vila* and *llar/lar* (house, in the sense of *home*).

- According to Coromines, 'vila' comes from the Vulgar Latin word vīla, which comes from the Classic Latin word VĪLLA, meaning 'villa', country house: "residence of the ambassadors when they were not admitted to Rome".
- Also according to Coromines, 'llar/lar' comes from the Latin LAR, "each of the family deities that inhabited a chapel at the entrance of the house and were often kept in a niche above the chimney".

I offer the following (alternative) explanation: *villa* comes from VI + LLA, 'union of lives'. And *llar* literally means 'union' or, with the meaning of repetition given by the <r>, '**re**-union space'.

This meaning of *villa* as 'union of lives' is also found in *vivienda* (dwelling), *vital*, *vivir* (to live)... In several languages *villa* means 'town'. In Occitan: *vile, viel, viele, vielle*. In French: *ville, vilage*. In Portuguese: *vila*. In Italian: *villa*. In Catalan: vil·la. In Basque: *villa, herri*. In English: *village*. In Romanian: *vilă*. Except in Latin, where it does not mean a settlement but 'country house'. Let us not forget that in Catalan the town hall is still called '*Casa de la Vila*'. And what does the Spanish word *ayuntamiento* (town hall) mean, if not 'union'? (Note: in Old Spanish, the verb *ayuntar* meant 'bring together').

We note therefore that the formant L/LL behaves as a relational determiner; it is, in fact, a true article at the end of the word, and proof of this is that it has survived in words mentioned above, like *davantal/davant* and *palmell/palma*, where the Catalan word shows a more archaic form than Spanish. This postponed article works exactly like the encyclical Romanian article: *tatăl* (the father), *omul* (the man). Subsequently, when the semantic relation between the formants was lost, the article was duplicated, placed in front of the word and assigned the same gender. The words that carry the masculine determining article 'el' maintain at the end the enclitic article <-el>, while the words that carry the feminine determining article 'la' end with the enclitic article <-la>. Here are some examples:

- el mart**ell**, l'an**ell**, el fus**el** (in Spanish, *el martillo, el altillo, el fusil* – in English, the hammer, the loft, the rifle)
- la bo**la**, la ra**lla**, la cisa**lla** (in Spanish, *la bola, la raya, la cizalla*– in English, the ball, the dash, the shear)

The suffixation of the determining article to the right of the noun was probably generalized in former stages of the Romance languages; interestingly, these constructions have survived in Romanian.

Regarding the indefinite article, in Romance languages its use is extensive, accompanying the noun. In Classical Latin, the numeral adjective UNUS was used but only with the indefinite value of *some*.

A note regarding Basque: it too places determiners (demonstrative, definite and indefinite quantifiers) as deictics to the right of the noun: *etxea* (the house). The equivalent of the article would be <-a> in singular and <-ak> in plural. Again Basque coincides partially with Hungarian. The definite article in Hungarian is placed before the word and does not mark the plural: *a/az* (in Spanish, *el, la, los, las* – in English, the); it only changes form depending on whether the following word begins with a consonant or a vowel.

And another note: Greek also has definite articles, which are equivalent to the Spanish ones.

Everything we have noted so far about the nominal forms (noun, adjective) seems to indicate that, in proto-Romances, there was no nominal case inflection. The grammatical function was indicated by the determiners and the pronouns. In modern Romanian, the persistence of a definite article to the right of the noun, which is duplicated in other Romances that currently add it to the left, would show that case markings were not lost in an alleged evolution from Latin to Vulgar Latin, but they simply did not exist in the proto-Romances, which seems to indicate, once again, that modern Romance languages would come from an older common parent tongue, and that this tongue was not inflectional but agglutinative in nature.

6.7 Verbs

Some of the characteristics of the morphological verbal paradigm in Romance languages are:

- Preferential use of periphrastic versus synthetic constructions.
- Different structuring of tenses.
- Different structure and little use of the passive voice.
- Absence of deponent verbs.
- Only three non-personal forms (infinitive, gerund and participle).
- Auxiliary verbs: SER, ESTAR (to be) and HABER (to have).
- Absence of absolute ablative constructions.
- Absence of infinitive sentences.

The verbal forms in Latin had three different aspects: present (present, imperfect and future tenses in the indicative and subjunctive modes), perfect (perfect and pluperfect in the indicative and subjunctive modes), and supine. This morphological distribution has no equivalent in the Romances, which form their tenses based on the thematic vowel, with tense and modal suffixes and personal endings dividing tenses into simple or compound.

At a phonetic level, these morphological changes mark a different stress pattern. There is also a profound restructuring of the verbal tense system, based on a different notion of time, i.e. its value has been changed through a lexical-semantic shift. Finally, there is also a change in the correlation and use of tenses between the main and subordinate sentences, so differences also exist at a syntactic level. In summary, Latin and Romance verbs show fundamental differences at four grammatical levels: phonetic, morphological, lexical-semantic, and syntactic.

At a morphological level, one of the important changes is the use of the participle for the creation of compound tenses along with the auxiliary verb *haber* (to have). These tenses, which require the presence of a participle, did not exist in Latin. Thus, in Spanish: *yo he amado* (I have loved) vs in Latin: AMAVI; *yo había amado* (I had loved) vs in Latin: AMAVERAM.

Another change may be found in the construction of the future. In Latin, the imperfect future was analytical and formed on the root of the present tense, adding the ending BI (first person BO, first and second conjugation), in Spanish: *yo cantaré* (I will sing) vs in Latin: CANTABO; or the ending E (first person A, third and fourth conjugation), *yo diré* (I will say) vs in Latin: DICAM. The future perfect was also analytical and formed on the root of the perfective aspect, to which the morpheme -ERI (first person ERO) was added. It is therefore very interesting to note that, in Medieval Latin and in areas where the proto-Romances were spoken, these tenses were written with periphrasis from the infinitive DICERE HABEO and CANTARE HABEO, at the origin of the present forms *diré* (I will say) and *cantaré* (I will sing).

Classical Latin did not have the conditional tense either. The explanation provided by historical grammar is that the conditional is formed by periphrasis from the infinitive, through forms such as CANTARE HABEBAM, which evolved to form *cantaría* (I would sing). Again, the question is how were the Romance languages able to all converge into such an original solution? They could have chosen any other option, as it happened in English, a language again similar to Latin in that the conditional tense. Unlike Romance languages, English developed a complex system known as 'modal verbs' to express up to three degrees of condition: true, possible, and hypothetical.

As for Romanian, the system of verbal modes and tenses is much more complicated than in any other Romance language. It is interesting to note that, since the 19th Century the tenses, have been simplified. For example, the current present perfect and pluperfect have an analytical (non-compounded) form that mysteriously resembles more the Latin form. However, if we go back, we find that ancient Romanian used periphrastic forms identical to those in Spanish. Let us look at some examples collected by Larisa Budai.[121] The fragments show the periphrastic forms of imperfect and pluperfect in ancient Romanian:

---

[121] Larisa Budai, a PhD student at the University of Iași, presented the lecture *The Bible from Bucharest versus King James' the Holy Bible* in Literature, Discourse and Multicultural Dialogue (2013). Information provided by Mihaela Alda.

Imperfect:

Ancient Romanian	Şi Moisi **era păscînd** oile lui Iothor, socrul său.
Modern Romanian	Şi Moise **păştea** oile lui Ietro, socrul său
Spanish	Y Moisés **estaba pastando / pastaba** las ovejas de Jetro, su suegro
English	And Moses was grazing the sheep of Jethro, his father-in-law
Ancient Romanian	Şi **era** norodul **cîrtind** rău înaintea Domnului
Modern Romanian	Şi norodul **cârtea** rău înaintea Domnului
Spanish	Y el pueblo **estaba protestando / protestaba** delante del Señor
English	And the people were protesting before God

Past Simple:

Ancient Romanian	Şi **fu auzind** sluga lui Avraam cuvintele lor
Modern Romanian	Şi **auzi** sluga lui Avraam / Avram cuvintele lor
Spanish	Y **estuvo oyendo / oyó** el siervo de Abraham sus palabras
English	And the serf of Abraham was hearing/heard his words

Pluperfect:

Ancient Romanian	**N-au fost venit** după îndulceţurile acealea
Modern Romanian	**Nu veniseră** după dulceţurile acelea
Spanish	No **habían venido** por esas golosinas
English	They hadn't come for those sweets

Ancient Romanian	Toți aceștea **au fost luat** muieri striine
Modern Romanian	Toți aceștia **luaseră** femei străine
Spanish	Todos estos **habían tomado** mujeres extranjeras
English	All of them had taken foreign women

Periphrastic forms in Romanian have also been attested at a synchronic level. In a recent paper by Veronica Chinde,[122] the use of periphrastic forms in the Banat dialect is analysed,[123] confirming that the two modalities (synthetic/analytical) coexist in many of the investigated areas.

The differences in the verbal paradigm regarding Latin are not limited to the appearance of new verbal tenses, a change in the temporal value of some forms or the use of periphrasis instead of synthetic forms. The syntactic correlations between the main and the subordinate sentences are also altered and follow different patterns:

- In Latin, the time correlation depended on the action expressed in the subordinate sentence with respect to that of the main action.
  - Present/future: if the action of the subordinate sentence happened simultaneously, the present was used; if the action expressed antecedence, the perfect was used; if the action had not happened, and therefore the relation was one of posteriority, the present of the active periphrastic was used.
  - Past: if the action of the subordinate happened simultaneously, the imperfect was used; if the action expressed antecedence, the pluperfect was used; if the action had not happened, and therefore the relation was one of posteriority, the imperfect of the active periphrastic was used.

  That is, verbal tenses were fixed according to a time relative to the main action and not in an absolute way, in relation to the actual time.

---

122 CHINDE, VERONICA. *Observații asupra realizării sintetice vs. analitice a mai-mult-ca-perfectului în subdialectul bănățean*. In *Dacoromania, serie nouă*, IX – X, Cluj-Napoca, (2004-2005), pp. 221-228. Information provided by Mihaela Alda.

123 A region in southwest Romania and northern Serbia.

- In Spanish, the main sentence is expressed in the indicative mode, and the subordinate in the subjunctive mode.[124] In addition, each temporal situation requires a specific correlation of tenses, for example:

Main sentence		Subordinated sentence	
Present indicative	*quiero*	Present subjunctive	*que vengas*
Future indicative	*esperaré*	Present subjunctive	*hasta que llegues*
Present perfect indicative	*me ha gustado*	Present perfect subjunctive	*que hayas ido*
Past imperfect indicative	*no esperaba*	Past imperfect subjunctive	*que vinieras*
Past simple indicative	*no creí*	Past imperfect subjunctive	*que fuera tan tarde*
Pluperfect indicative	*no me había parecido*	Pluperfect subjunctive	*que se hubiera enfadado*

The simple forms of the Latin passive voice were synthetic and were formed from the same themes of the active voice but with special endings. Forms such as AMABATUR or APERIUNTUR had their equivalent in proto-Romances with the periphrastic forms AMATUS ERAT and SE APERIUNT. On the other hand, the passive, as abundant in Latin as in English, is a less frequent formation in the Romances, which, in addition, do not have a single deponent verb.[125]

Latin had the following non-personal verb forms:

- 6 infinitive forms: present, past and future, active voice and passive voice;

---

124 In Romanian, the subjunctive is called 'conjunctiv'. It is used much less than in Spanish or even in French. Many concordances are made with the verb in the indicative (Mihaela Alda).

125 Deponent verbs are those used in Classical Latin with meaning in the active voice, but whose conjugation is done in the passive voice.

- 3 participle forms: present, past and future; and
- 1 gerund, which declined in four cases.

One of the ways used by Latin to create subordinate constructions was by using infinitive sentences with a subject in the accusative – a structure that has not been found in the Romances but was common in English. This has already been discussed in the chapter on *Similarities between Romance Languages*. Another typical structure in Latin was the absolute ablative, a participle in ablative that was equivalent to an adverbial subordinate.

In the Romances, non-personal forms are reduced to the present infinitive, the past participle, and the gerund. Latin used the verb ESSE as an auxiliary verb. In Spanish, we use the verb SER (to be) to form the passive voice. For the active voice, we use the verb HABER (to have). In Catalan we have the auxiliary verbs *ser* (to be, archaic use), *estar* (to be), *haver* (to have), *anar* (to go, periphrastic past perfect formation). The verb *ir* (to go) is also used as an auxiliary in French (and, by the way, also in English), for constructions that indicate movement in the future. Romanian uses the verb *a fi* (to be) for attributive, locative and existential sentences.

Romance languages have a high combination of verbal periphrases: modal (obligation, necessity, probability), and aspectual (inchoative, durative, repetitive).

Finally, we would like to make a remark about verbs in Basque, whose paradigm is very complex. There are personal and impersonal forms, both simple and compound, with several auxiliary verbs that present many irregularities. There are six modes: indicative, imperative, conditional, potential, hypothetic, and votive. The passive conjugation is the usual form, although there are also transitive and intransitive conjugations. There is no accusative case because the direct object is used as a subject: this relation is called ergative. An important fact is that, although there are some synthetic verbs in Basque, most of the verbs use periphrastic forms (participle of the conjugated verb plus the form of the auxiliary verb). The Basque verb is like a summary of all the components of the sentence and has in itself a reference to the direct object and the indirect object. Moreover, it uses postpositions that can be placed after the root and after the endings of the cases. This ascription to the grammatical cases avoids ambiguity, allowing more freedom in the order of the elements:

Antonio cogió el bastón Antonio took the walking stick	Andonik hartu zuen makila Makila hartu zuen Andonik Hartu zuen Andonik makila
y saludó a los amigos and waved to his friends	Eta agurtu zituen lagunak Eta lagunak agurtu zituen Eta zituen lagunak agurtu

6.8 Non-inflected forms: prepositions, adverbs and conjunctions

In Romance languages there are three closed grammatical categories. They are called 'closed' because the linguistic resources of composition and derivation do not allow for the creation of new elements. In addition, they do not have the inflection, i.e. they cannot be modified and do not offer formal variation or alternation of either gender, number, person, tense or any other of the variables characterizing the other five inflected grammar categories: nouns, adjectives, pronouns, determiners and verbs.

The three closed categories are:

- Adverbs
- Prepositions
- Conjunctions.

The words in these categories are functional: they give meaning to the text more than the words that contribute the content. In a way, they are the fundamental words of the language, and for this reason they are not modified. Connectors provide information on the inner workings of a language, and thus of the mind. The preference of the Romances for periphrastic solutions and for phrasing over analytic constructs must be significant. It cannot be explained satisfactorily as stemming from Latin, and deserves to be studied carefully.

> In all three closed categories (adverbs, prepositions and conjunctions), there is no relation of continuity between Latin and Romance languages. Although they should be the most stable elements, there are no formal equivalences. If Latin were the parent tongue of the Romances, it should have transmitted its linkers and connectors to its daughter tongues. However, what we find is a complete rupture.

According to Professor Mark Pagel and to what I have discussed in the chapter on *The sluggishness of linguistic change*, the words most frequently used are indeed the ones that change the least: these words can last, with very few modifications, not only for centuries but for millennia. In the list included in the mentioned chapter we have seen that the words most resistant to change were some determiners and adverbs.

Functional categories are used much more frequently than lexical categories. Therefore, it appears surprising that those categories that are the most resistant to change are also the most distanced from Latin.

6.9 Adverbs

Characteristics of adverbs in the Romances:

- Absence of adverbs in <-ter> and <-e>
- Modal adverbs in <-mente> with periphrastic formation of degree
- Differentiated paradigms for adverbs of place, time, quantity, affirmative and negative, and interrogative.

Adverbs constitute an invariable, and generally closed, category. They are specifiers of verbs, of adjectives or of other adverbs. They can form intransitive propositions. We are dealing with a grammatical category that appears to have undergone a radical change when related to Latin.

In Latin, most modal adverbs were formed from an adjective. Adjectives with three terminations added the ending <-e>, and those with one and two terminations added the ending <-ter>.

adjective	adverb
TIMIDUS	TIMIDE
FORTIS	FORTITER

The neuter accusative singular of some adjectives like MULTUM (*much*) and PAULUM (*little*), neuter ablative singulars such as FALSO (*falsely*) and other forms in <-am>, <-im> and <-itus> were used as adverbs.

As with adjectives, the comparative and superlative degrees of the adverbs were formed synthetically, by adding <-ius> and <-issime>:

adjective	adverb	comparative	superlative
DOCTUS	DOCTE	DOCTIUS	DOCTISSIME
wise	wisely	more wisely	very wisely

Romance languages do not use Latin adverbial endings. All Romances (Spanish, Catalan, French, Provençal, Italian) have applied an identical criterion for the formation of modal adverbs, by adding <-mente> to the adjective. The official explanation is that, after abandoning the Latin endings, the Romances had to invent another solution. Once again, it is striking that the Romances were so unoriginal in 'inventing' an identical construction.

In Latin, adverbs of place were formed by joining an interrogative pronoun (UBI, QUO, UNDE, QUA) and a demonstrative (HIC, IDEM, IS, ISTE, ILLE), a relative (QUI) or an indefinite pronoun (QUICUMQUE, ALIQUIS, ALIUS). That is to say, depending on where the speaker was located, the space relation could indicate the place where he was (UBI), the place where he was going (QUO), the place where he had come from (UNDE) or the place he was passing through (QUA); this person or thing was the subject referred to in the first person HIC (this), in the second person ISTE (that), or in the third person ILLE (that one). All this could become more complicated when referring to something previously mentioned: IS (this) + UBI (where) gave the IBI form (there where we said). Below is an example to illustrate this complex correlation:

ISTE	UBI + ISTE = ISTIC	QUO + ISTE = ISTUC	UNDE + ISTE = ISTINC	QUA + ISTE = ISTAC
that	there (where you are)	there (towards where you are)	from there (from where you are)	around there (around where you are)

Fortunately, there is nothing similar in the Romances, because at this point we would no longer know if we were going or coming from anywhere (UNDECUMQUE).

Latin adverbs of time – with few exceptions like HODIE (today), HERI (yesterday), ANTE (formerly), POSTEA (after) – are also unparalleled in the Romances. However, let us see what happens if we compare them:

LATIN	Spanish	Catalan	French	Italian	Romanian	English
CRAS	mañana	demà	demain	domani	mâine	tomorrow
CREBRO	a menudo	sovint	souvent	spesso	adesea	often
DIU	mucho tiempo	molt de temps	longtemps	molto tempo	mult timp	a long time
ETIAM	además	a més a més	en outre	ulteriore	de asemenea	also
MOX	pronto	aviat	bientôt	presto	în curând	soon
NUNC	ahora	ara	maintenant	ora	acum	now
NUPER	hace poco	fa poc	récemment	recentemente	recent	recently
OLIM	en otro tiempo	temps enrere	autrefois	una volta	cu mult timp în urmă	once upon a time
PROTINUS	inmediatamente	tot seguit	tout de suite	immediatamente	imediat	immediately
RURSUS	de nuevo	de bell nou	encore	di nuovo	din nou	again
SAEPE	a menudo	sovint	souvent	spesso	de multe ori	often
SEMEL	una vez	una vegada	une fois	una volta	o dată	once
STATIM	enseguida	tot seguit	aussitôt	immediatamente	imediat	immediately
TANDEM	finalmente	per fi	enfin	finalmente	în sfârșit	finally
TUM-TUNC	entonces	llavors	alors	allora	atunci	then

Romance languages show a tendency to use composition, adverbial periphrases, and the lexicalization of adverbial propositions which can include nouns, adjectives and verbs. Similarities are observed between languages, alternating solutions in a comparable way in one case or another, but always moving away from Latin. For its part, Romanian does not have the ending <-mente> for adverbs.

Regarding affirmative or negative adverbs, Latin had no affirmative adverb corresponding to our *yes*. To answer affirmatively, the verb of the interrogative sentence used to be repeated (see the chapter on syntax) or else an affirmation of the following type was used:

ITA, ETIAM	thus	SALTEM	at least
VERO	truly	CERTO	surely
SANE	certainly	SCILICET	undoubtedly
EQUIDEM	really	IMMO	rather

The adverb *no*, which (according to Mark Pagel) would date back 15,000 years, existed in Latin in the form NON. Its first form was NE, which was only preserved in compounds and as an enclitic interrogative particle (see *Syntax*). Another negative adverb was HAUD which was a specific word, not used to negate a sentence. It seems that it stopped being used due to its homonymy with AUT (conjunction *or*).

To lend a negative meaning to a sentence, indefinites were used such as NEMO (no one), NIHIL (nothing), NULLUS (none) NEUTER (neither); and the negative adverbs MINUS (not completely), NUMQUAM (never), NUSQUAM (through nowhere), NEQUAQUAM (by no means), NECUBI (nowhere) and the emphatic negative MINIME (nothing at all). There were also phrasings like NEQUE...NEQUE (neither...nor), NE...QUIDEM (not...not even), NON...IAM (no...no longer).

Contrary to what happens in Spanish, in Latin two consecutive negatives were equivalent to an affirmative. The meaning differed, depending on the order in which the elements appeared.

nemo non	everyone	non nemo	someone
nihil non	all	non nihil	some
nunquam non	always	non nunquam	sometime
nusquam non	everywhere	non nusquam	somewhere

In other cases, the use of several negatives in the same sentence did not lead to an affirmative, but was rather there to lend emphasis. According to some grammarians, in Latin negatives responded to expressivity criteria, whereas in the Romances their use is grammaticalized.

6.10 Prepositions

Prepositions form a non-inflected and closed category. There are simple prepositions, compound prepositions, and prepositional phrases. Their function is of transition or union; hence, so they require a nominal syntagma. Unstressed prepositions (in Spanish *a, con, de, en, por*– to, with, from, in, for) have grammatical meaning. Stressed prepositions (all others) also have some lexical meaning.

Latin case endings could not express all the relations of place and direction, so Latin also required the use of prepositions. These were synthetic particles with multiple values. Although they always introduced verbal complements, some of them governed the accusative and some others the ablative.

Accusative prepositions				Ablative prepositions	
AD	to, toward, near, until, for	OB	for, because of, before	A, AB	from, since, as of, by
ADVERSUS	against, towards	PENES	held by	CORAM	in the presence of
ANTE	facing, before, in front	PER	through, during, because of, thanks to	CUM	with
APUD	at the house of, next to	POST	behind, after	DE	of, on, about
CIRCA, CIRCUM	around	PRAETER	against, except, aside from	E, EX	from, coming from, depending on
CIS, CITRA	on this side of	PROPE	near	PRAE	compared to
CONTRA	against, opposite	PROPTER	on account of, because of	PRO	for, on behalf of

Accusative prepositions				Ablative prepositions	
ERGA	towards	SECUN-DUM	throughout, according to	SINE	without
EXTRA	outside of, other than	SUPER	above	Accusative and Ablative prepositions	
INFRA	under	SUPRA	over	IN (Ac.)	in, to, towards, against
INTER	between	TRANS	across, on the other side of	IN (Abl.)	in
INTRA	within	ULTRA	beyond	SUB (Ac.)	below
IUXTA	beside	VERSUS	against	SUB (Abl.)	under

Many prepositions are recognizable because they have been used in the creation of neologisms and literary words; therefore, in the Romances they are formants and do not exist as independent prepositions. For example, TRANS is part of the word *transoceanic* but we cannot say *"we have passed trans Madrid*. Instead, we say *on the other side of Madrid*. Of all the prepositions included in the table above, only one third have an equivalent in Romance languages. Hence, it is easy to appreciate the preference of our languages for prepositional phrasings that combine two or more prepositions with other words. There are many more – but here are some examples: *a falta de* (in the absence of), *en aras de* (for the sake of), *a juicio de* (in the opinion of), *como consecuencia de* (as a result of), *a bordo de* (on board of), *por espacio de* (for a period of), *a efectos de* (for the purpose of), *en cuanto a* (as for), *sin opción de* (without the possibility of), etc. The particularity of these phrasings is the fixed order of the words that form them; they have merged and have a single meaning. However, their grammatical function is that of a syntagmatic connector and they act exactly like a simple preposition.

Let us now focus for a moment on the preposition 'de' (of), which introduces the genitive construction.

Joseph Greenberg's[126] universal linguistic principle number 2 states: "In languages with prepositions, the genitive almost always follows the governing noun, while in languages with postpositions it almost always precedes that noun".

In all Romance languages, the genitive construction follows the noun: noun + preposition 'de' + genitive construction. On the contrary, Latin placed noun complements before the noun, and the genitive construction in particular was expressed with the genitive case.

These are different linguistic typologies. The structure of the noun complements in Latin resembles the Saxon genitive in English. This model definitely diverges from Romance languages.

6.11 Conjunctions

Conjunctions also form a non-inflected and closed category. They are the ties that bind compound sentences, whether by coordinating or subordinating.

One of the most difficult issues to explain is why Romance languages do not have the Latin resources to establish meaningful relationships between different units. For example, of the many Latin conjunctions used as coordinating links, the Romances only use the following:

ET	i/y (and)	copulative coordination
NEC	ni (nor)	negative copulative coordination
AUT	o (or)	disjunctive coordination

Only three conjunctions? No wonder the process has been labelled as a loss through vulgarization! In Latin, the total inventory of conjunctions was huge and had complex semantic nuances, correlations, varying degrees of overemphasis; some were enclitic, others had a formal variation depending on whether the next word began with a vowel or consonant, or preceded a stressed word... First, let us look at the Latin conjunctions used to link phrases by coordination: copulative, disjunctive and adversative.

---

126   See footnote 106, page 98, in this book.

Coulative coordination	
ET, AC, ATQUE, -QUE	and
ETIAM, QUOQUE	also
NEC, NEQUE	and not
NE... QUIDEM	neither...not even
ET... ET	either...or
CUM... TUM	not only...but particularly
MODO... MODO	either...or
TUM... TUM	either...or
NEQUE... NEQUE	neither...or
NON MODO... SED ETIAM	not only...but also

Disjunctive coordination	
AUT, VEL, -VE, SIVE, SEU	or

Adversative coordination	
SED, AT, AUTEM, VERUM, VERO	but
TAMEN	however

There were also conjunctions to emphasize a statement in another sentence:

Causative coordination	
NAM, NAMQUE, ENIM, ETENIM, QUIPPE	therefore, since, indeed

And there were even copulative illative or conclusive conjunctions indicating the effect or consequence of an earlier statement:

Illative coordination	
ERGO, IGITUR, ITAQUE	so
QUARE, QUOMOBREM	thus, whereby
PROINDE	therefore

As for the subordinate relationship, in Romance languages subordinate clauses play a complementary role equivalent to the function of a noun, an adjective or an adverb – so they are often divided into substantive, adjective, and adverbial clauses.

Latin equivalents are clearly the same in the case of the adjective subordinates, because in both cases relative pronouns are used. It is the only subordinate clause that presents a perfect equivalence.

Subordinate noun clauses could be formed in different ways:

- With an infinitive sentence and the subject in the accusative;
- With direct interrogative pronouns;
- As an indirect interrogative sentence
- With conjunctions QUOD, UT, NE QUIN, QUOMINUS; and
- Without conjunction, with the verb in the subjunctive.

Latin expressed the adverbial subordination through one of the following procedures, or with both of them simultaneously:

- Using a subordinating conjunction; and
- Using the verb in subjunctive or infinitive modes.

The same subordinating conjunctions could be used with different functions and values, since this depended on the context. However, in the Romances the opposite is true: it is the conjunctions that indicate if the clause is a temporal, comparative, final, conditional, consecutive, causative or a concessive subordinate. The most common Latin conjunctions were:

\multicolumn{2}{c}{Adverbial subordination}	
UT	as, when, that, because, although, though, so that...
CUM	when, whereby
QUOD	with regard to, yes but, that, whereby, in spite of, even though, similarly to...

These conjunctions could be translated with very different values, depending on the context. For example, CUM could be an ablative preposition or a conjunction with temporal value (when) if the verb of the subordinate clause was in the indicative, or it could form a construction known as HISTORICAL CUM if the verb was in the subjunctive (equivalent to a gerund or a composed gerund, according to whether the verb was in the imperfect or the pluperfect).

As for QUOD, it could introduce an adjective relative clause, a substantive subordinate clause (that), or a causal adverbial clause (because). Finally, one of the greatest difficulties for students of Latin is how to translate a sentence introduced by UT: in Spanish, for example, such a sentence can be equivalent to a substantive subordinate clause or a temporal, comparative, final, consecutive or concessive adverbial clause. How would one know? In Latin it depended on the verb tense, on the type of verb, or on whether the main sentence had a demonstrative (pronoun or adverb) in correlation with the conjunction...

What is really important to understand is that it is not a matter of changing a particular conjunction, or that a specific Latin structure could not have any equivalent in the Romances. What we are trying to explain here is that the whole system is altered: even the temporal correlations between the main and the subordinate clauses correspond to a different grammatical concept.

For example, to express a purpose, we use *para que* (for) and other equivalent expressions such as *a fin de que, con el objeto de* (so that, in order to...). In Latin, however, a purpose could be expressed in five different ways:

- UT + subjunctive;
- Supine in accusative;
- AD + gerund in accusative;
- QUO + comparative; and
- Relative pronoun + subjunctive.

For a temporal clause, the following conjunctions could be used:

- UBI + indicative verb (when);
- UT, SIMUL, AC, STATIM AC + verb in indicative (as soon as, after that);
- POSTQUAM + verb in indicative (after that);
- CUM + verb in indicative (when) or in subjunctive (temporal value with causal nuance);
- ANTEQUAM, PRIUSQUAM + verb in indicative or subjunctive (before that); and
- DUM, DONEC, QUOAD + verb in indicative (while, until) or in subjunctive (temporal value with an idea of intention).

Temporal constructions could also be constructed with a participle.

The behaviour of conjunctions in the Romances has nothing to do with their behaviour in Latin. The two patterns are completely different. Furthermore, the Romance languages contain no trace of the structures introduced by the Latin conjunctions: *ac, at, autem, cum, donec, enim, ergo, etiam, etsi, igitur, itaque, nam, ne quin, quidem, sed, sive, tamen, ut, vel*... Why is that? If we copied the vocabulary, why didn't we do the same with the relational elements? The three non-inflected and closed grammatical categories are indeed essential for structuring the language properly.

> The historical grammar books at University are trying to explain this significant absence by saying that, due to their inability to understand each other, speakers of Vulgar Latin (the same ones who lost cases and conjugated verbs incorrectly) ended up in parataxis, communicating through gestures: they shook their heads to say yes or no, they shrugged their shoulders...
>
> Did they have to gesticulate because they did not know how to use a few conjunctions and instead were able to conjugate the 60 forms of the indicative tenses, plus the 36 forms of the subjunctive, as well as the imperative and the nominal forms of the verb?

In the 19th Century, 90% of the Spanish population was illiterate and yet everyone conjugated verbs properly and organized sentences with perfect correspondence between subject and predicate. Nobody dropped the subjunctive or confused a conditional with an imperfect. These are concepts invented by grammarians! Speakers apply innate grammar rules without having to know them; speaking well comes naturally.

There is not a culture in the world, nor in the remotest tribe hidden in the most faraway forest, that does not have a fully developed language. Every language in the world, every single one of them, can perfectly resolve communicative nuances; all languages can express abstract concepts and complex feelings, and even if people are illiterate and have never heard of grammar, they use it naturally because, as evidenced by generative grammar, language is part of our human condition. However, we admit that non-verbal language is very expressive and conveys inputs of great importance at subliminal levels, but it does not replace spoken language because the latter is part of cognitive processes and, as already mentioned, we cannot structure our thoughts without language!

If Romance languages do not use Latin connectors, how does this affect the syntax?

6.12 Syntax

Some of the main features of the Romances' syntax are:

- Absence of syntactic function markers (declensions)
- Absence of Latin linkers
- Tendency to lexicalize prepositional, conjunctions and adverbial phrasings and clauses
- Changing the order of the sentence constituents
- Structure of interrogative sentences.

As noted when discussing languages in contact and the creation of inter-languages (creole), syntax is the only part of grammar that does not allow hybrids. Changes always take place based on one of the two languages in contact. Therefore, if the syntax of the Romances is not Latin, what language does it come from? What language influenced Latin speakers to the point of altering their language and wiping out its syntax?

It is the syntax of this parent tongue that we seek, because syntax encompasses all linguistic levels: phonetic, lexical-semantic, morphological. It is difficult to understand why the Romances, which copied the vocabulary, did not do the same with the relational system and the grammatical markers of Classical Latin. On the contrary, linguists' explanations refer to a paratactic state of grammar illiterates. This is very strange and must be significant.

6.13 Absence of syntactic function markers (declension)

We are told that, as the nominal case system was no longer sustainable after successive phonetic changes, Vulgar Latin became an inflected language with more synthetic than analytical forms, where the word order became a necessary element for the syntactical coherence of sentences.

However, it is not true that the order of sentence elements emerged as a 'necessity' resulting from the absence of case markings. It must have been the other way around. Joseph Greenberg's universal linguistic principle number 41 states: "If in a language the verb follows both the nominal subject and the nominal object as the dominant order, the language almost always has a case system". This principle describes precisely the syntactic structure of Latin, which placed the verbal objects before the verb. In Latin, the verb was always at the end of the sentence, which made it 'necessary' for the grammatical function to be indicated by case markings.

In my opinion, the proto-Romances had no case markings simply because they did not need them. The Romances are verbal-framed languages, where the verb usually occupies the central position. It is not easy to change this order because it affects the structure, the self-organizing system and the cognitive processes that establish semantic hyper-incursions.

We know that the scribes who wrote in Latin did not think in Latin. They spoke and thought in another language, where the order of the constituents of the sentence was fixed, as evidenced in the texts written in Medieval Latin with a sentence structure that uses 'our' word order. Thus, a Latin sentence that sounded like:

> ANTONII MENSAM TIBI DONO
>
> Genitive construction + DO (accusative) + IO (dative) + verb (first person singular present tense of the indicative)
>
> appears written in medieval texts as:
>
> DONO MENSA DE ANTONIO A TE
>
> Verb + unmarked noun (DO) + preposition DE + unmarked name (for the Genitive construction) + preposition A + pronoun in dative (IO)

What does this simple sentence tell us? It clearly transpires that the scribe tried to write in Latin (a dead language that he did not master) while he thought and spoke in a Romance language. Therefore, even if the words are Latin and it sounds like Latin, it is not Latin. The reorganising of the constituents shows that the syntax is typical of a Romance language!

Let us look in more detail at what the change in the order of sentence constituents entails.

6.14 Change in the order of sentence constituents

Classical Latin sentence construction placed the verb at the end of the sentence and the adjective and other noun complements before the noun. It readily admitted hyperbaton and transpositions, so it was very common to insert additional terms between two terms linked by semantic or grammatical relations.

> S + O + V   Subject + Object / verbal complement + Verb

Joseph Greenberg's universal linguistic principle number 13 states: "If the nominal object always precedes the verb, then the verb forms subordinate to the main verb also precede it".

This is exactly what we find in Latin.

Thus, in Latin, subordinate clauses always preceded the verb of the main sentence.

On the contrary, the word order in the Romance languages is essentially fixed, and the usual order with transitive verbs is Subject-Verb-Object.

> S + V + O   Subject + Verb + Object / verbal complement

Thus, in the Romances, the verb of the main sentence is usually placed in the central position, while the subordinates are placed in end positions.

Joseph Greenberg's universal linguistic principle number 15 states: "In expressions of volition and purpose, a subordinate verbal form always follows the main verb as the normal order, except in those languages where the nominal object always precedes the verb".

In Latin, the nominal object always precedes the verb. Not so in the Romances.

From what we have noted so far, the sentence structures in Latin and Romance languages belong to different linguistic typologies.

Moreover, this does not only happen in the sentence structure. An identical distinction can be made in noun phrases. Romance languages prefer putting the modified words and their modifiers together, i.e. the determiner precedes the noun, but the adjective and the prepositional complement go after the noun:

> N + NC   Noun + noun complement (NC)

This order is not accidental because the adjective does not have the same meaning if it is placed before the noun; it acquires an affective value and even a different meaning. Thus, we can see that, in Spanish, *un hombre pobre* (a poor man) is not the same as *un pobre hombre* (a mean-spirited man); or, in another example, *una cazadora deportiva* (a sports jacket) is not the same as *una deportiva cazadora* (a hunter sportswoman).

Joseph Greenberg's universal linguistic principle number 19 states: "When the general rule is that the descriptive adjective follows the noun, there may be a minority of adjectives that precede the noun. But when the general rule is that descriptive adjectives precede the noun, there are no exceptions".

Once again, we find that Latin and Romance languages belong to different linguistic typologies.

6.15 Interrogative sentences

In Latin, a question was expressed by joining the enclitic interrogative particle <ne> to the word on which the question fell; and this word was placed at the beginning of the sentence. If a negative answer was expected, NUM was used, meaning *perhaps?*

The verb in the interrogative sentence was in the indicative, as if the sentence was assertive. Only when one wanted to include a hint of doubt or deliberation, the verb would be in the subjunctive.

An affirmative answer to a question was expressed by repeating the verb or word (without affirmative adverb), or with the particles ITA, ETIAM, VERO, SANE. If the answer was negative, the verb was repeated placing the word NON before it, or using the adverbs NON, MINIME, MINIME VERO. For example:

	Question: VIDISTINE REGEM? (Did you see the king?)		VIDISTI + NE
Affirmative answer	VIDI SANE	(yes)	verb VIDI adverb
Negative answer	NON VIDI MINIME	(no)	NON + verb VIDI adverb

Latin used interrogative pronouns when the question fell on a single element of the phrase: QUIS? (who) QUID? (what) UTER? (which one of both) UBI? (where) UNDE? (from where) CUR? (why). In case of a double question, UTRUM or NE was used in the first element, and AN in the second (and if this element was negative, ANNON).

As we can see, it was difficult to ask questions in Latin! These patterns have nothing to do with Romance languages, which mark questions with a melodic curve and a rising tone at the end of the sentence.

Let us consider an example provided by Yves Cortez,[127] where we can examine how, in all Romances, questions are formed identically. Indeed, Latin is the only language that stands out:

Latin	Musica**ne** delectaris?			
French	Tu	aimes	la	musique?
Spanish	Te	gusta	la	música?
Catalan	T'	agrada	la	música?
Italian	Ti	piace	la	musica?
Romanian	Îți	place		muzica?

Joseph Greenberg's universal linguistic principle number 8 states: "When a yes-no question is differentiated from the corresponding assertion by an intonational pattern, the distinctive intonational features of each of these patterns are reckoned from the end of the sentence rather than from the beginning".

Indeed, we see that this principle applies to all Romance languages. But not to Latin.

---

127 CORTEZ, YVES. *Le français ne vient pas du latin!* L'Harmattan Editions (2007), p. 98.

CONCLUSION

Where do Romance languages come from?

The above analyses converge to one conclusion: Romance languages did not come from anywhere. They were already here. They were the idioms spoken, more or less, on their territories of today, with slight differences according to their linguistic and geographical distance.

The LINGUA LATINA was the language spoken in Latium and was closely related to the ROMANA LINGUA and to its neighbours' idioms in the Italian peninsula, the Iberian Peninsula and the historical Dacia. The contingents of Roman settlers who moved to the Iberian Peninsula came from central and southern Italy, so they spoke Sabellian languages such as Oscan and Umbrian – not Latin.

The Western Roman Empire fell in the 5th Century. The Eastern Byzantine Empire continued for another ten centuries, until the fall of Constantinople in the hands of the Turks (1453). Throughout this period, the importance of Latin in Western Europe was exceptional because it was the language of power and culture. Latin was the only written language. And yet, in some legal texts, we can glimpse the existence of a different oral language. This allows us to confirm the existence of the Romances as perfectly structured spoken languages in medieval times.

The case of Romania sheds a new light on this process: the Romans occupied less than a quarter of the territory of ancient Dacia, for just 165 years. With respect to the Romanian language, no intense Romanization factors occurred: Latin was not a scholarly language because Romanians were Christian Orthodox: in their Orthodox Church, for many centuries, the ritual language was Slavonic. Therefore, the fact that in Romania a Romance language is spoken on a much larger territory than was ever occupied by the Romans, and that this language converges with Western Romance languages, without having been in direct contact with these for at least two thousand years, suggests a common parent tongue, older than Latin.

As shown in recent research, on a morphosyntactic structure level, linguistic change is a very slow process. Some of the most common words in the current vocabulary could be traced back to the Palaeolithic era. Cognitive linguistics is changing basic concepts of linguistics by postulating a symbolic basis for all grammatical constructs. These structures are made up of information conglomerates put together to form units used by speakers in order to understand and produce language.

Hence, we should stop viewing language as a combination of grammatical structures and start considering symbols as its basic units - these units being the pairing of a semantic structure with a phonological label.

What we find is that there is a meaning —a metaphysical philosophical idea— hidden in the words.

To deepen this new concept, we have discussed toponymy to discover some formants of this ancient language that have survived in the vocabulary of the modern Romances. This research leads us to consider that such lexemes are the sound representation of symbolic elements which allow us to unveil the way of thinking, feeling and living of its speakers. When people share similar cultural and social elements, when ideas are the same, the results are formally related words (lexemes). This is why (and how) similarities between languages come about.

Romance languages share a high percentage of phonetic, lexical, morphosyntactic and semantic characteristics, showing a close kinship to a linguistic typology that relates them to each other but distances them from Latin. Therefore, the articulatory characteristics that (according to historical grammar) are attributed to the shift from Latin to Vulgar Latin and then to Romance languages might have evolved directly from a common, previous language, without having to justify this development through Latin. The relationship between Romance languages and Latin would then be that of kinship and not filiation.

It is certainly fascinating to see that Romanian retains some aspects that help us get closer to this common parent tongue. It has been said that all Romance languages, daughters of Latin, lost their grammatical cases during the degenerative process from Latin to Vulgar Latin. The different tongues were de-structured to such an extent that the speakers came to parataxis, whereby gesticulation was needed in order to be understood. The case opposition preserved in Romanian was considered an archaic feature that had survived the evolutionary process. We have shown this is not so. In Romanian, nouns have no case inflection; it is the article, located to the right of the noun, that carries the case markings. On the other hand, if Latin had no article, how can Romanian cases be considered a feature of Latin heritage? Furthermore, suffixation of the definite article to the right of the noun was widely used in the earlier stages of the Romance languages, and this is the origin of the constructs that have survived in Romanian. I also wish to emphasize that case endings do not show nominative-accusative opposition, but rather nominative/accusative versus genitive/dative, which is very different, because this seems to set them apart from the Indo-European pattern of nominative-accusative opposition. I have also discussed derivational suffixes, showing that this compositional feature indicates an agglutinative, non-inflected language which must be much older than Latin.

Regarding the written documentation, in the Iberian Peninsula and as evidenced by the *Aljamiado* texts, Mozarabic was spoken, a Romance language similar to Galician and Catalan. With the rise of the kingdoms and the creation of cohesive urban centres in various territories, the Romances became separate, giving birth to Galician, Leonese, Castilian, Navarro-Aragonese and Catalan. Diachronic studies show how, from the 13th Century onwards, these languages evolved, expanding –or reducing– their territories. The language territories were reduced when the speakers stopped using their languages, yielding to the predominance of Castilian.

How far back can we go to discover the earliest Romance languages? The settlers established in the Iberian Peninsula spoke Iberian languages. Despite having more than two thousand epigraphic texts discovered on all sorts of supports and archaeological contexts, Iberian writing has still not been deciphered. However, this work could open a new avenue of research if we manage to prove that many of the changes that historical grammar attributed to the evolutionary process from Classical to Vulgar Latin could be caused by the substrate language, the phonetics and morphosyntax of the language or languages from which the Romances stem.

Peoples established around the Mediterranean were part of the same *koiné* and spoke related languages. The archaeological context challenges any theory of large migrations and shows a housing continuum from the Mesolithic and often even earlier, dating from the Palaeolithic, and nomadic societies. As long as populations moved about and mixed together, languages maintained an affinity to some degree.

Our current languages share many words. This affinity does not respond so much to the incorporation of foreign words or to a bizarre phonetic evolution but to a common vocabulary based on the same ideas or symbolic concepts expressed through compositional formants that point to an older common parent tongue, shared by the various Mediterranean peoples, a language which must date back thousands of years. These differences would arise, following a slow natural evolution, from sedentarism and isolation.

In light of all this, I believe it is wrong to force a degree of kinship of Romance languages to the point of stating that they are in a direct relation of filiation with Latin. Because the phonetics and morphosyntax of the Romances do not share a linguistic typology with Latin, we must focus our attention on previous languages; in the case of Spain, on Iberian.

What do we know about the Iberians? The importance of their legacy has been ignored and yet the Iberian period bequeathed us the territorial distribution of the towns, the sacred places of worship, the economy based on agriculture and cattle raising, the staples of our diet, the design of agricultural tools, the framework of social relations between the rural and the urban worlds, the weekly markets, the trading nature, the curiosity and openness to new cultures. Two thousand five hundred years later, we can still find in our lifestyle the characteristics of a population that spoke and wrote in their tongue during the same period as the proto-Hellenic peoples. During all this time, Modern Greek has not evolved so much from Ancient Greek; they are different, but understandable. And what about us? What do we know about Iberian? Why has their writing not been deciphered? Why do schools keep explaining that the Roman conquerors brought us culture and civilization? Why don't we learn about the high level of an indigenous culture that since ancient times traded with other Mediterranean peoples, such as the Minoans, Mycenaeans, Greeks and Phoenicians? In linguistics, why has such a complicated theoretical framework of phonetic evolution through external influences been developed, regardless of the articulatory features derived from Iberian? Why does historical grammar disregard the fact that Iberian writing has a high distribution of palatal vowels, responsible for more than 50% of the changes attributed to the lenition phenomenon? Why is it not known that Iberian distinguished two sibilants, two rhotics and had the same vowel distribution as the Romances? Too many questions!

Unfortunately, this study is being concluded with more questions than answers. This shows that we must profoundly rethink the current theoretical basis of philological studies. Progress in this discipline will not be possible if we keep ignoring the culture and languages before the Romanization process, the substrate at the base of all subsequent changes.

The Iberian language is our great hope. We will have to wait for the publication of new studies that will allow us to further decipher Iberian writing.

Printed in Great Britain
by Amazon